PREPARE TO BE MOONSTRUCK

THE
ENCHANTED
MOON

The ultimate book of lunar magic

STACEY DEMARCO

THE ENCHANTED MOON

The ultimate book of lunar magic

ROCKPOOL

A Rockpool book
PO Box 252
Summer Hill
NSW 2130
Australia

rockpoolpublishing.co
Follow us! **f** ⓞ rockpoolpublishing
Tag your images with #rockpoolpublishing

ISBN: 9781925946147
Published in 2021 by Rockpool Publishing
Copyright text © Stacey Demarco 2021
Copyright images on pages 6, 30, 40, 60, 74, 172, 184, 205 © Sam West 2021
Copyright design © Rockpool Publishing 2021

Edited by Brooke Halliwell
Cover design by Dana Brown, Rockpool Publishing
Design by Sara Lindberg, Rockpool Publishing
Images from shutterstock
Author Photo by Stu Nairne

NATIONAL
LIBRARY
OF AUSTRALIA

A catalogue record for this
book is available from the
National Library of Australia

Printed and bound in China
10 9 8 7 6 5 4 3 2 1

This book is dedicated to Jo, Miranda and Wanda – the power of three.

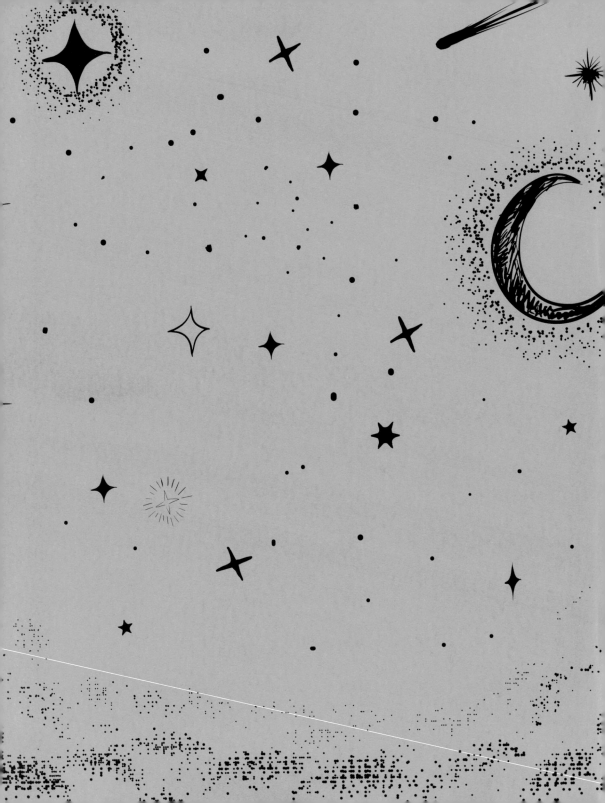

CONTENTS

PREFACE

There is a saying in French that describes the time of twilight as '*entre le chien et le loup*'. It means 'between the dog and the wolf'. At the time I learnt of this saying, I was indeed sitting within the dusk, the sun having gone down, the moon just peaking over the horizon, the colours turning gently and determinedly towards the deep blues of youthful darkness.

The description of the twilight in this way made my heart leap a little, as personal truths sometimes do, because I have always seen the night and of course the rising of the moon as something just that much wilder than the light of day, a different animal entirely, although somehow related.

Here in the darkness, under the moon, I have always thought there was a freeing of oneself, a chance to transform into a somewhat richer, truer version of my daytime self. Here was a space of mystery and possibility and a place to cast an incantation and indeed listen to the wolves howl.

Whilst there are lots of reasons our ancient ancestors loved the moon for magic, this feeling of contact with a wilder self is surely an important one.

I have loved the moon since I was a child, just as I fell in love, hopelessly in love, with the natural world and the ancient world of mythos. I was a bookish child more interested in learning about the deeds and lessons of gods and goddesses and wonderment of magical animals than I was the shows on TV but also saw this same magic in the natural world around me. In the earliest photos of myself I am with dogs, cats, plants, gardens. Eventually, in a profoundly convoluted journey, I found a pagan spiritual path (pagan = earth honouring) and specifically, the way of the Witch.

It felt like home. It felt like I was born to do this.

I have been writing about the natural cycles of the moon (and the seasons) for a number of decades now and teaching about them for longer – yet, I was slightly apprehensive about writing a book like this because I wanted it to be truly useful and authentic for as many people as possible.

The difficulty here is that with *real* magic – YOU are the magic. YOU are the weaver, the conduit, the conductor. YOU are part of the sacred alchemy of what you are creating.

And all of the variety of YOUs out there makes a one-stop-shop cookie-cutter approach pretty impossible.

So, I have decided to share what I know with you in the same way as I teach – in a way that is non-prescriptive. I'm going to suggest and guide but it will be you who will create the magic. I will certainly not spoon-feed you. I will not push or present one tradition or one way. Instead, I will give you magical skills that will hopefully empower your life and the lives of those around you and open you to further enquiry and advanced work if you choose.

I will give you lots of frameworks in which lunar workings can be performed and many spells, rituals, meditations and 'ceremonies' I have created, tried and tested but I'll also give you the tools to weave your own.

This is real power.

And did I also mention that all this can be really pleasurable, joyful and fun? (Well, I just did.)

So, come with me, friend, and let us play in magic and *liberte* under all those moons 'entre le chien et le loup.'

STACEY DEMARCO

THE MOON IS
FOR EVERYONE

Recently, one crisp winter's night at about 3.30 am, my dog Malu woke me up asking to go outside to toilet. This was unusual, as she normally sleeps right through.

So I got up with her and let her out. This night, it was a full moon so everything was bathed in that bright, silvery blue light and you could see the garden and surrounds lit up almost like daytime. It was so light that we cast a shadow as we stepped through the door to the open verandah and garden.

But Malu stopped on the verandah and looked up. She was so still. I went out with her and there, spread before us, was the full moon in line with the planets Jupiter and Saturn. One, two, three: hanging like jewels in the sky. We both just stood there watching.

Everything was totally quiet except for the hiss of the sea. She stood close to me and I placed my hand gently on her big head and we clearly had a moment under that universe.

After a while, the cloud came drifting across the sky and the moon and planets were hidden. Malu, then and only then, silently padded off the verandah into the garden. I waited for her under that incredible sky, cold as I was, and checked all the talismans I had out for blessing under the moonlight.

After a time, she rejoined me and stepped inside, with not a look upwards, not even considering the sky because the clouds were still there.

All of us get moonstruck, even those of us who don't come in a human package.

So like this, I invite you to go outside on a clear night. Look up.

Hopefully, you'll see the stars a-twinkling. If you are really lucky you might see the swirling Milky Way spilling across the darkness. And then, there she is, the big moon unmistakeable in her glory and power.

She moves the earth itself, stabilises it into orbit. She releases and pulls the seas. She is the object of devotion, the inspiration of poems, the realm of goddesses and she has witnessed the very first of us rise up on two legs and venerate her.

Generation after generation, we have stood barefoot under the same moon, wishing, setting intentions, dancing and drawing her graceful power.

You, it is said, are made of the very same swirling matter that is the stuff of stars, yet it is the moon who, as we will see, gave you a chance to develop as a species. The you that is human but also the you who is pure possibility, changing constantly, renewing and transforming.

Take a breath under that moon and take this moment to recognise that power and rejoice in it for your next step is the precursor to your future self.

It's all heady stuff, yes?

But we humans have been connected to the moon spiritually since we first stood up. Moon worship is so old we are still going backwards in time in our discoveries.

For example, the fine crescent of the new moon is an ancient symbol that stretches back to prehistory. There are cave drawings featuring crescent moons, sculptures of goddesses with crescent-mooned diadems, and the goddesses Aphrodite, Hekate, Diana, Artemis, Inanna and many central Asian female deities who were often depicted with new moon symbology. Go back even further, into the cave paintings of the Neolithic, and moon (and sun) symbology features along with symbology relating to moon-based phenomena like tides and the female menstrual cycle.

The knowledge that nature was rhythmic and cyclic was something known and observed by early humans. The moon cycle wasn't something just beautiful (although of course it is!) but it was also useful. Useful in telling time, knowing the birth time of babies, knowing how animals related to it (for hunting, hiding, mating) and for the harvest of plants.

The moon was intrinsically linked with survival and the spiritual health and connection of the tribe.

Millennia later, I do not think much has changed. Whilst our needs may have changed somewhat, the moon cycles still are linked with our spiritual and physical health and our connection between people no matter where they live.

THE

SCIENCE

Why Knowing About the Moon Scientifically Enhances Our Workings

If you have bought this book, you would definitely have expected magic and a kind of spiritual theme to the information. Yes, that is here. But, as a pagan, I am most interested in the way 'what is' weaves with the magic of 'what can be', for we are a little more grounded than most (excuse the pun).

I believe that the forces that actually exist and are described by science – those evolutionary forces, elemental phenomena like electricity, gravity, dark matter, pressure, magnetism and the areas of physics and astronomy – certainly are important components to the alchemy of magic.

Everything is connected to everything else. Energies and forces, building upon each other, step by step, ingredient by ingredient, swirling and weaving in powerful alchemy, creating a synergistic whole so much more powerful than the sum of its individual parts. The earth and the relationship with its moon shows us the universe is heaving and dancing with elemental aliveness, with deep connectivity, with an electric creativity.

This is why I will give some concise scientific-based information that can assist you in the formulation of strong magic and positive physical and mental transformation. So let's start big. Let's start with the beginning.

So there is a Big Bang...

The Moon is Life

The universe begins to expand and in our own galaxy planets begin to swirl and form.

When the earth as a planet and its moon were developing, the earth was unstable. It regularly wobbled on its axis. This made the earth's atmospheric and surface conditions dangerous and not particularly conducive to life.

As the moon formed, its gravity actually gave Earth a stability that it needed to bring consistency to its chaotic climate and ecosystems. This stability and gravity enabled seasons to begin to cycle, weather to be somewhat predictable, and the earth less likely to wobble on its axis.

This gave life, as we know it, a chance to begin and evolve.

So, stop right there and take that in. The lunar cycle isn't just one of waxing and waning, or even one that just affects the tides on Earth, it is mega.

It is part of our whole evolution as living beings.

The moon's effects are flowing through our DNA and life on Earth. In magic, this makes the moon a force to be engaged with and not ignored in our workings and weavings. Bringing balance and stability to our physicality on Earth is no small thing.

The Contrast

The moon, of course, has no atmosphere. That's right, none of that blue transparent auric blanket of protective gases. The surface of the moon is therefore unprotected from powerful cosmic rays and solar winds, and has no huge variations in temperature. It's pocked with craters from meteorites great and small because there is no atmosphere to burn up the incoming. The lack of atmosphere also means no sound can be heard on the moon – so no birds singing or cicadas humming even if they could live there. And if you were standing on the moon, the sky would always appear black.

I think in some ways this contrasts to our own planet glowing with life, resplendent with sound and so vulnerable. It is something of the attraction of the big glowing orb, and it's worth remembering just how alive our planet is, just how special our earth is when other planets and moons are so uninhabitable to us. Yet without the moon, especially in the beginning, our planet would not have formed the stable core that it did, as you now know. Lunar, solar and 'earthy' work together.

In magic, this is the same.

Consistency

The moon always shows the same face to us. As it cycles through the phases and its face looks more or less visible to us, the side that faces us doesn't change. This is because the moon rotates around its axis in exactly the same time it takes to orbit Earth.

This constancy and consistency gives us a model for ourselves. It is good to know that our ancient ancestors stood under that same moon and saw her same face, to know that we are not completely different from them. That we, as humans, still pretty much require the same things to make us safe and happy.

This gentle consistency helps us retain our fidelity and resilience.

The Tides

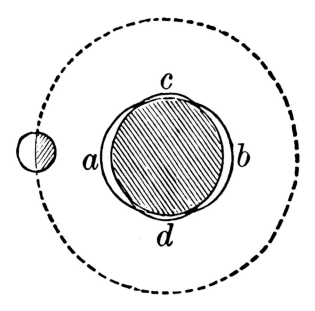

The moon has its own gravitational force. The moon's gravitational pull generates tidal force. The tidal force causes the earth itself – and its water – to bulge out on the side closest to the moon and the side farthest from the moon. These bulges of water are referred to as high tides. The moon causes high and low tides on the sea and large bodies of water.

Since the tides are linked closely to the movement of the moon, we use them as powerful forces to help us weave particular kinds of magic. Just as the moon's various phases direct energy, so does the pull and flow of the sea.

Simply check the tide charts in the newspaper or on the coast guard internet sites, or there are apps you can download which will give you this info in real time. I confess I am quite the Luddite and I have a beautiful analogue 'tide clock' which sits in my kitchen which I consult more often than not.

High Tide or Tide Coming In

The incoming tide is great for 'calling in' something or increasing something. For example, you could cast a spell or do a ritual on a high tide for bringing prosperity to you, increasing your health or calling in a new love.

Some suggestions:

O Asking for natural flow

O Building partnerships

O Asking to move forward with something or something to move towards you – attracting a new relationship

O Increasing intimacy

O Attracting fertility and a child

O Travel

Low Tide or Tide Receding

The low tide is perfect for taking energy out and reducing the power of something.

Some suggestions:

O When you wish to diminish something that is a barrier

O Cutting cords to release old trauma

O When you wish to reduce the power of problem people – negativity, resentment

O For saying goodbye to bad habits or old patterns

O Shame reduction

O Asking for the natural flow of rest, relaxation, pause

O Letting anything go

On super full moons the tides are very extreme and are called king tides. Use these opportunities well! They are wonderful for calling in prosperity and, in particular, business.

The Light

Science has determined the earth's geomagnetic field varies according to the moon phase and therefore has consequences, but has neglected to study the same effects on the human body and any consequences we may have.

However, it is possibly the body's reaction to the more intense light that perhaps has the greatest physiological effect. Whilst in ancient times, night was naturally dark and we had no electric lights as we do now, it was easy to allow the body to work in simpatico with the lunar cycles. Now, this is more difficult and our bodies find it hard to adjust.

When we dream we are experiencing deep REM sleep. If you are disturbed by the strong light and energy of the full moon, then you may well wake when you are in the middle of the dream, remembering it when normally you may not.

You might also not sleep as well, or you may sleep more deeply during the extreme moons of dark or full – this, of course, can impact on the quality and quantity of your dreams.

The media now heralds every visible eclipse and every super moon as a time to go out with a picnic blanket with your buddies and watch. Consciously or not, we get joy out of watching something so beautiful and beyond ourselves. Here is something still wonderful and awesome that can only do us jaded techno-junkies a whole lot of good.

LUNAR RHYTHMS AND CYCLES

Waxing and Waning

The moon has always been one of the strongest symbols of the feminine divine and of the goddess. The way the moon changes over the sky each night is a keen reminder of the power of change and of the natural cycles inherent in our world and within us. This is soothing psychologically and physically. We were born to be aligned with these cycles.

For me, even the simple action of looking up and connecting with the moon each night (even if it is cloudy) links me directly with my own power as a woman and certainly my powers of creation.

The Witches' Way sees the moon in three main aspects traditionally, and these aspects describe stages in the natural life of any goddess. The three stages are that of Maiden, Mother and Crone. Each of these stages is different energetically and symbolically.

The maiden aspect of the goddess is waxing, growing in size and power in the sky after the dark moon. The mother aspect is when the moon is at its creative peak, at full moon. As she diminishes and grows darker, we see the face of the wise elderly crone. These three stages reflect our own life cycle closely. We are born and grow, we mature and create (not necessarily children), and we will eventually grow older and die.

The idea of working with the moon is to go with the flow of these cycles not against them. As you track yourself against the changing face of the moon, you will begin to know when you feel high or low energy, when you feel introverted or extraverted. Knowing which moon and which aspect to use to strengthen particular intentions is useful wisdom.

For me, the rule is as the moon gets smaller in the sky, the energy wanes. As the moon gets larger again, the energy increases. Reducing energy means we get to reduce things or rid ourselves of them. Increasing energy in contrast is about attraction and growth.

Here is a summary of the phases of the moon and the influences that each phase brings to our unconscious and more sensitive psychic selves.

Full

- The moon is full in the sky
- Full energy!
- Often a time when people find it hard to sleep or sleep extra deeply

- ○ Dreams are often more vivid and easily remembered
- ○ Should you set intentions during this moon, it gives you high impact results, and is perfect for attraction spells of any type
- ○ Great time to explore finding your true path and purpose in life
- ○ Psychic skills are often heightened but often not so good for sleep!

Waning

- ☾ The moon is growing smaller in the sky – after a full moon and before new moon
- ☾ Energy is reducing
- ☾ Good time to set intentions with a purpose of getting rid of something that no longer serves you or to reduce an obstacle
- ☾ Great time to give up a bad habit e.g. any addiction, any limiting or negative belief

New or Dark

- ● No moon visible in the sky
- ● Traditionally a time of introversion and rest
- ● Good time to set intentions that ask for peace and creative flow
- ● Experienced practitioners can use this deep energy for powerful healing
- ● Psychic skills are often heightened

Waxing

- ☽ The moon is growing larger in the sky – after the new moon and before the full moon
- ☽ Energy is growing and expanding
- ☽ Good time to set intentions with a purpose and intention of growth and moving towards something you desire

- Wonderful time to ask for more money, more positive relationships, and better health
- Wonderful for prosperity spells
- Perfect for asking for body vitality, a pay rise, a new job, more recognition

OTHER MOON PHENOMENA

There are a few other moon phenomena worth mentioning when it comes to the weaving of science and magic.

Eclipses

A lunar eclipse is when the earth passes between the sun and the moon and a shadow is cast on the moon. It can only happen on a full moon.

A solar eclipse is when the moon passes between the sun and the earth – causing a shadow to project onto the earth's surface. Both kinds have been noticed by ancient peoples, astronomers and astrologers and written about and observed extensively.

Often they were portents of ill luck or signs that the gods were engaged and watching for particular reasons.

In paganism, eclipses are usually a signal to go within and pay special attention to what is happening. We are asked to assess or to understand that energies can be wild and chaotic and so we look to the balance. It's a powerful time for certain kinds of magic. I like making protective amulets particularly on lunar eclipses. In astrology, eclipses often denote significant events will happen in someone's chart or that unexpected things may occur. Depending on what zodiac sign the eclipse is in, the attributes of that sign may be sublimated or magnified.

Blue Moon

In old farmers' almanacs, a blue moon was described as the third full moon in a season that has four full moons. The newer and now more accepted description is that a blue moon is when there are two full moons in one calendar month. Either way, it is a rare occurrence and has inspired the saying 'Once in a blue moon' when describing an event or behaviour that happens rarely.

The energy and power of blue moons can be best taken advantage of by setting intentions on these moons of things that you really want but have never felt could happen. I refer to big wishes! The 'almost' miracle stuff that we would be both delighted and surprised if it manifested.

This is the time for big, unexpected magic!

Super Full Moon

A 'super' full moon is a moon that is on its closest approach to Earth in its revolutions. It is also referred to as a 'perigee' moon. This full moon looks huge in the sky and, being so close to the earth, it influences the oceans more than usual, causing more extreme tides than normal.

These changes in gravity and force are certainly noticeable, yet for most people who follow the cycles of the moon and do magical workings aligned with them, it is the energy of these super full moons that are most important.

If a 'normal' full moon gives us an opportunity to have rocket power under our intentions, a super full moon greatly magnifies this energy into a super nova.

We all, if we are growing, want to attract experiences into our lives. This can be positive relationships, a lifestyle that suits us better, clarity, love, prosperity, creativity... the list goes on. So super full moons are useful in pulling in 'big' ticket items... the new relationship, that big job, a baby.

OUR MIND AND BODIES AND THE MOON

The idea of working with the moon is to go with the flow of the cycles not against them. Know how you, in your body, react to different cycles. This is a personal thing. Not everyone gets energised by a full moon, for example, particularly if they are born on a waning cycle or dark moon – more on that soon.

We are moon-influenced animals even if most of us don't go howling under it! Within long-held knowledge, there are a number of ways that it's believed the moon impacts our physical bodies.

The Light Effect

There is more light in certain phases of the moon cycle. The brightest being full moon and the least light at dark moon. It is possibly the body's reaction to the more intense light that perhaps has the greatest physiological effect.

Think of what life was like in ancient times before light was available at the flick of a switch and we had ambient light in our streets all the time. The night was naturally dark and we had no electric lights to glow as we do now, and the brightest object in the sky was the moon. It was easy to allow the body to work in simpatico with the lunar cycles. Now, this is more difficult and our bodies may find it hard to adjust!

Our bodies need light – yes, even moon light – to work well and for our moods and bodily functions to be balanced. Women, for example, have a hormone in their body called luteinizing hormone (lute is latin for light) which triggers successful ovulation. This hormone needs light to be produced effectively and to do what it needs to do.

There is evidence in some ancient cultures and within some oral traditions passed down that women were encouraged to have sex on and around the full moon (full power, most light) if they wished to conceive (or have a balanced cycle) and then have their moon days on the waning/dark moon times (release, letting go, starting again). (The human menstrual cycle is approximately as long as the lunar cycle).

Now there are some peer-reviewed studies which show people do experience less sleep during full moons; however, anecdotally, it is insomnia or highly disturbed sleep around the full moon that is heard about most from all kinds of people all over the world.

Many shamans choose the full moon for journeying and it is said that the Amazons ran wildly to exhaustion during full moons in order to cleanse and purge their spirits. Modern witches use the full moon as their Sabbath time and certainly many do prophetic dream work during this phase and on that of the dark moon too.

Mood

We have all heard of the terms lunatic and lunacy – both words with a moon based essence – and there is a lot of talk and discussion around whether the lunar cycle influences our behaviour.

Some studies agree – we even have some police forces rostering on more officers on those full moon nights – and some say there is no correlation between mood and the moon.

Ask most paramedics or hospital-based doctors and nurses and they certainly notice an increase of activity on full moon nights. The Lunar and Seasonal Diary I write each year has a popular audience in medical people – they want to know when the full moons are on to avoid being rostered!

Maybe it is another 'light influenced thing' but people are more extraverted and go out more under the full and fuller moons. It might also be the influence of water in our bodies due to the extremes, we are not sure scientifically, but the jury is certainly not out anecdotally.

So what I advise is that you keep a journal or diary of not only your magical work but your moods and anything like poor sleeping patterns or an increase in appetite. This way, you can observe for yourself how (or if) the moon affects you. Watch every moon. Connect with every moon – remember the first three skills I mentioned. This way you can ride the beautiful certainty and calm of the cycle.

If it does, then you can do something about it by preparing and seeking to balance those moods ahead of time. Being forewarned is forearmed!

Body Balance

We encourage everyone to love their incredible bodies and to treat them with respect and love and to nourish them. So when a client might come to me asking me to help them lose weight or someone wishes for weight loss during New Year's resolutions, then I explain it will be a spell for balance I'll be giving them, not weight loss.

Setting your intention and beginning your body balance programme on the full moon is best. This gets the mind used to the idea that this is a great idea and something you want. You might even cast a spell for health and vitality that night to boost it along.

Waning Moon: Begin your programme straight after full moon and notice that the moon is waning, taking with it extra weight and fluid. You will lose weight more rapidly during a waning moon.

New Moon: When the moon reaches new moon, we again do a ritual to boost our intention. Lighting a candle and simply asking the universe to continue to assist you to reach your goal and to achieve greater health is enough.

Waxing Moon: We must be careful here not to eat foods that are not aligned with our intention, as waxing moon cycles will hold them to the body far more than during waning cycles. However, we generally have more energy during waxing moons, so this is the time to boost your activity levels and burn off what you consume more easily.

Full Moon: Be grateful for what you have achieved (or achieved so far) and set your intention moving forward.

Glorious Hair!

I know many of you already love cutting and growing your hair by the moon cycles, and I know that full and new moon days are some of the most popular days in hairdressing salons all over the world! It is thought that different phases influence hair growth just like they influence tides, so it's no surprise that full and waxing moons are your best friends if you want longer locks.

Growing your hair

Traditionally, should you wish to grow your hair, only cut it when it is in its most active phase during the full or waxing moon.

Keeping it similar length

If you wish to preserve your haircut (very handy for those who have a fringe or short hair), cut your hair on a waning moon.

Strengthening

For giving your hair treatment days, you might try new moon days and waxing moons.

For the mother of all good hair days, go for the full moon in Cancer for all your conditioning and cutting treatments.

For hair removal

Whether you wax, laser or shave, the best time to take that hair off is in the waning moon cycle.

INNER

CYCLES

The lunar return:

Across a number of ancient cultures like the Egyptian and Sumerian, it was believed that the moon phase upon birth triggered the beginning of life and remained as a person's peak time energetically throughout life. This was especially evident for women as it determined her most fertile time.

Records of Sumerian medicine indicated a belief that a woman is most fertile when the moon is at the same phase as her birth. Ancient Celts and Egyptians recorded the moon phase at birth and told both sexes when they came of age. This is more an astronomy concept than an astrological one.

We call this a lunar return.

Up until fairly recently, the accepted science was that human women had a covert cycle of ovulation. This means a hidden, set time usually at the centre of the cycle but with no overt clues like your dog and cat may show if they are in heat. Science says that there is only one small fertile time in a human woman's cycle and it has to be around that centre point. Now, latest research shows that there is some evidence to the contrary: that lots of exposure to sex/men can cause spontaneous ovulation at any time in the month. Further studies are now being undertaken to see if there is any pattern to this within diet and light exposure. So, perhaps old wisdom is true wisdom in this case!

If you are male, this includes you too! Scientists believe that men have a fertility biorhythm and it could well be related to light and frequency of sex also.

So, the simple idea of knowing which phase of the moon you were born on and noting it as well as keeping an eye on the moon regularly seems to induce more hormonal balance in both sexes. This is, of course, very useful if you are wishing to conceive.

If this doesn't interest you at this time, knowing when you will be feeling most vital and energetic really does have profound impacts in areas such as decision-making, work and certainly in physical endeavours such as endurance and sport.

For me, knowing my lunar return has been a revelation. Whilst I'm not interested in conception, what I am interested in is when I may be physically and mentally at my best.

I had always wondered why – especially as a witch – I felt very drained on full moons. After all, wasn't that meant to be the big night for a pagan like me? It wasn't that I was tired so much, it was that I didn't feel as extroverted as everyone else. I preferred to do solo rituals or group meditation rather than huge ceremony. I noticed there were others that were like that too.

So when I learnt about the concept of the lunar return and looked up the phase that was up in the sky when my mother birthed me, it wasn't that much of a surprise to see it was a dark moon that graced that night. Being born on a dark moon meant all the body's processes started at that time and so the cycle was strongest again when that came around. Dark moon was my superpower and full moon was dashed with a little kryptonite.

Now why is this useful to know? Well if I want to make an important decision or have a big occasion where I need to be at my best, I'll choose dark moon so I can be at my sharpest and best. I've also noticed I'm physically stronger at dark moon. I lift weights and keep records of my progress and I noticed I have a lot of personal bests around the darker time.

Now this doesn't mean I am necessarily fuzzy or weaker or anything nasty like that on a full moon. It just means that I shouldn't push myself too hard at that time. I have learnt to shape the way I do magic at full moon to both take advantage of that huge energy but not let it wipe me out (hint: I take a lot in and let the rest flow through like a conduit).

If you want to know your lunar return both NASA.com (yes, NASA) and timeanddate.com have historical moon charts online that you can conveniently look up to find your personal moon.

I thought I would add in an alignment meditation for those of you who might want to sync their fertility cycle with their lunar return moon.

Alignment Meditation for Women

This alignment is for those women whose lunar return date is not the same as their current 28-day moon cycle ovulation mid-point and they wish to combine them to identify a lunar hotspot (a super fertile time).

Best results are done at night right before sleep. I recommend lying in bed alone and relaxing and simply falling into sleep once the ritual is complete.

If you can see the night sky all the better.

Preparation

Know your lunar return phase and have a clear picture of what the phase looks like in your mind.

Know your estimated 28-day cycle ovulation point (roughly 13–14 days after day 1 of your moon bleed this month or if you chart your cycle when symptoms and temperature suggest ovulation occurs).

Record this meditation until you can remember it yourself.

Perform this spell any night on a regular basis and be certain to perform it on your lunar return phase.

Ensure that you will be undisturbed.

Casting

Open a circle around your bed if you wish although this is not necessary.

Light your candle if you are using one and relax.

Breathe in and out deeply. On the in-breath begin to take deep into your body the sweet energy of Mother Earth. Green, nourishing and never-ending healing. On your out-breath exhale any negativity or problems that the day you have experienced have brought. The day is over now, and it is time to breathe out any thoughts or circumstances that do not serve your needs right now. Blow them out and allow them to be recycled by the Mother. There is time enough tomorrow to look again with fresh eyes and wisdom at these.

Continue to do this until you feel at ease and at peace on every level. Allow this. Take your time.

Now when you are ready, begin to imagine that there is no ceiling above you, it is now the deep, comforting midnight blue of the night sky.

The stars are twinkling and they are everywhere. Not just on top of you but around you. You are floating on a sea of stars, indescribably beautiful. You are totally relaxed and connected.

You look down at yourself reflected in the stars' silvery light and you know that yes, you are a goddess and creator. You now begin to look deeper through your soft body that softly twinkles in the starlight. You now look inside yourself at your yoni and your creative system. You see how your ovaries look like a dandelion, full of healthy and growing eggs. They look just like the seeds on the dandelion, perfect and full of potential.

Now you communicate with your body and ovaries.

> *"My eggs are my essence. They are perfect and fertile. They will unite and create."*

Now look into the night sky again. There, in front of you, is your lunar return moon phase.

It is getting larger in the sky as you look at it. It is all encompassing and you feel a great love of your own body and personal power as a woman looking at it. This is a symbol of power for you.

Now again turn to your dandelion-like ovaries and eggs.

Communicate to your body:

> *"When the moon looks like this in the sky, the time is right to be ripe and to release. The date for this to happen is (**insert your lunar return date for that month**). Union is certain as I am irresistibly fertile."*

Now imagine one egg being born from the ovary (like a seed blowing from the dandelion) and it looks just like your moon. Watch it travel gently down the fallopian tubes where it glows even more brightly. Suddenly there are many tiny sperm surrounding your egg. You know these have come healthy and masculine from your partner (or donor) and one burrows into your egg. You watch as both the Divine Feminine and Divine Masculine combine to create a glowing spark full of life and energy. You watch as this form attaches itself to your womb and is enveloped there.

Communicate to your body:

> *"I welcome this baby of the moon. It is the best of both of us and will be born easily into this world. It will be healthy and happy as we will."*

Hold on to this pleasurable feeling as you joyously move through the night sky basking in your moon.

Know that conception is close.

The goddess and god are close and will assist you.

Now and only when you are ready, come back to the comfort of your bed and let the room become more concrete.

Breathe deeply and settle down to sleep.

Know that the universal goddess and the god have heard your desire to align cycles. Know that your mind and body are already responding. Your cycles are aligning. Close your circle if you opened one.

Alignment Meditation for Men

This alignment is for those men who wish to boost their sperm count and motility of sperm on their own lunar return or further boost it around their partner's lunar return.

Best results are done at night right before sleep. I recommend lying in bed alone and relaxing and simply falling into sleep once the ritual is complete.

Preparation

Know your lunar return phase and have a clear picture of what the phase looks like in your mind.

Know your partner's estimated 28-day cycle ovulation or lunar return date and phase.

Record this meditation until you can remember it yourself.

Perform this spell on any night on a regular basis and be certain to perform it on your lunar return phase.

Ensure that you will be undisturbed.

Casting

Open a circle around your bed if you wish although this is not necessary.

Light your candle if you are using one and relax.

Breathe in and out deeply. On the in-breath begin to take deep into your body the sweet energy of Mother Earth. Green, nourishing and never-ending healing. On your out-breath exhale any negativity or problems that the day you have experienced have brought. The day is over now, and it is time to breathe out any thoughts or circumstances that do not serve your needs right now. Blow them out and allow them to be recycled by the Mother. There is time enough tomorrow to look again with fresh eyes and wisdom at these. Think now also of the god – He who is protector and ruler of masculine fertility. He assists you to let go of issues that really are not important and to focus on your wish for a child.

Continue to do this until you feel at ease and at peace on every level. Allow this. Take your time.

Now when you are ready, begin to imagine that there is no ceiling above you; it is now the deep, comforting midnight blue of the night sky.

The stars are twinkling and they are everywhere. Not just on top of you but around you. You are floating on a sea of stars, indescribably beautiful. You are totally relaxed and connected.

You look down at yourself reflected in the stars' silvery light and you know that yes, you are a god and creator. You are strong and virile, and you feel powerful in your masculinity. You now begin to look at your lingham as it glows in the starlight. It is erect and hard. You now look inside yourself through your testicles at your creative system. You see how millions of sperm are being made every second. Take a closer look. They are all healthy and strong. Every second as you watch more are created, more than you could ever imagine, all strong with tails that kick energetically. Each and every one is perfect and full of potential.

Now you communicate with your body and testicles.

> *"My sperm are my essence. They are perfect and fertile. They are ready to unite."*

Now look into the night sky. There in front of you is your moon phase.

It is getting larger in the sky as you look at it. It is all encompassing and you feel a great love of your own body and power as a man looking at it. This is a symbol of power for you.

(If you wish to align your cycle with your partner's, watch now as the moon transforms itself into her lunar return.)

Now again turn to your body and sperm.

Communicate:

> *"When the moon looks like this in the sky, the time is right to be ripe, perfect and plenty. This will be the time to release. The date for this to happen is (insert your lunar return date for that month or the day you will try and conceive). Union is certain as I am irresistibly fertile and purposeful."*

Now imagine your sperm being released with complete ecstasy all travelling towards your partner's moon-like egg. Watch and be filled with wonder as many of your sperm, wave after wave, surround the egg, which is the essence of her. Now one of your sperm burrows into the egg. You watch as both the Divine Feminine and Divine Masculine combine to create a glowing spark full of life and energy. You watch as this form attaches itself to your partner's womb and is enveloped there.

Say:

> "In the name of the god, I welcome this baby of the moon. It is the best of both of us and will be born easily into this world. It will be healthy and happy as we will."

Hold on to this pleasurable feeling as you joyously move through the night sky basking in your moon.

Know that conception is close.

The goddess and god are close and will assist you.

Now and only when you are ready, come back to the comfort of your bed and let the room become more concrete.

Breathe deeply and settle down to sleep.

Offer your gratitude

Know that the goddess and the god have heard your desire to align cycles.

Thank the goddess and the god for being here with you tonight. Be grateful in the knowledge that all is as you have asked it to be, if it be their will and for the greatest good of all.

Know that your mind and body are already responding. Your cycles are aligning or strengthening.

Complete the ritual

Close your circle.

Extinguish the candles.

Sleep!

Participation

Begin to live what you have experienced. Ensure you share your progress with your partner, particularly if they are aligning with you.

THE MOON DOESN'T WORK IN ISOLATION

The lunar cycle is meant to be layered with other cycles, as we know all systems are connected, magical or not. One cycle I love to combine with the lunar cycle is that of the seasons, in particular the European seasonal festivals featured in the ancient Celtic Wheel of the Year.

Now how does this work? It's simple and complex! So certain seasons give off certain energies. For example:

Spring: Transformation, new beginnings, cracking open of the earth in fertility, beauty, growth, love, fresh starts.

Summer: Full extroverted energy, warmth, heat, joy, passion, masculine, full power, big growth.

Autumn: Transformation, letting go, dying back, reassessment, simplifying.

Winter: Introversion, solitude, rest, darkness, the void, fallow field, death, silence, planning.

For example, if I wanted to do a spell or ceremony for prosperity, a spring or summer full moon or waxing cycle moon would be really great timing.

If I wanted to let go of old trauma, a dark moon in winter would be optimal.

If I wanted to bless a new business for success, a new moon in spring or summer would be wonderful.

Now, if we add the magical layers of even more cycles of seasonal energy – one of the eight festivals of light vs dark, heat vs cold, death vs life... well then, our timing becomes even more powerful and our workings even more effective.

Importantly, these sacred times connect us with the light, the land and with the seasons. The land is our mother; She feeds us, shelters us, and gives us comfort and joy. The festivals give us a chance to give something back to her and honour all that She does. As modern people, we often forget this and feel disconnected without quite knowing why.

The continuous cycle lends itself to the image of a wheel. The ancient Celts and their predecessors saw time as a wheel or spiral divided by eight festivals as follows. Modern witches can use the 'themes' of each celebration to do magical workings of their own in complete synergy with the natural cycles. The dates featured on solstices/equinoxes change every year and are to be used as a guide only.

Samhain (Hallowe'en)

Southern 30 April Northern 31 October
- Celebration of death as a continuation of life
- Borders between the dead and living are not fixed and impassable
- The veil between the worlds are at their thinnest so one can ask the ancestors and spirits for guidance and communication on the future
- Celebrating where you came from
- Traditional time for scrying
- Witches New Year!

Yule (Winter Solstice)

Southern 21–23 June Northern 21–23 December
- Longest night of the year
- Mid-winter festival often linked to the Christian Christmas
- Archetypally linked with the birth of a child of promise and light: Dionysus, Arthur, Jesus, Baldur
- Celebrates the return of the sun and thus hope
- Abundance spells and charms
- Giving thanks and gifts of goodwill

Imbolc (Candlemas)

Southern 1 August Northern 1 February
- Celebration of light returning
- Goddess as Brigid (St Brigid)
- Fire festival
- Clarity and healing
- Light to shine, self-knowledge/creation

Ostara (Spring Equinox)

Southern 21–23 September Northern 21–23 March

- Night and day are equal, but moving towards summer
- Balance and growth
- Leave what you don't want and create the new
- Fertility and love
- New projects

Beltaine (May Day)

Southern 31 October Northern 30 April–1 May

- Marriage of the goddess and the god
- Maypoles – phallic and yonic symbolism
- Love magic (weddings/handfastings)
- Animus and anima/masculine and feminine balances

Litha (Summer Solstice)

Southern 21–23 December Northern 21–23 June

- Longest day, shortest night
- Sun is at its fullest power yet year begins to wane from here
- What brings light and joy into your life – develop this
- Self development
- Celebration of the masculine divine

Lammas (Lughnasadh)

Southern 1 February Northern 1 August

- First harvest – first loaf baked
- The god begins his journey into the underworld
- Sorrow and celebration
- Fruition, taking stock and harvesting what you have achieved

Mabon (Autumn Equinox)

Southern 21–22 March Northern 21–22 September

- Harvesting the main crop
- Take stock of what has served you well/what has not served you well
- What needs repairing before the dark comes
- Preparation for harder times
- Welcoming change of energy

Want to do workings for balance? Equinox festivals are perfectly matched with the moons closest to the date.

Want to do workings to attract love? Try Beltaine or Imbolc!

Want to change your life in a profound way? Samhain will give you the opportunity to let things die that you no longer need and Litha will grow something new.

Want to feel grateful and take stock of what you have? The harvest festivals of Lammas and Mabon will mosey that along.

WHAT DO THE ASTROLOGICAL SIGNS MEAN?

Separate to the meanings of the phases of the moon and the timings of the Wheel of the Year, there is also the layer of meaning often added where the moon is transiting within the signs of the zodiac. The moon makes a full transit of the earth (and the signs) every 2½ days.

I have listed over the page the astrological phases of the moon and some corresponding themes around which magical workings can be performed extra effectively.

Moon is in:

Capricorn

Excellent for magic concerning planning, clarity, strategy, career and purpose, status, obstacle busting.

Aquarius

Excellent for magic concerning popularity, strengthening friendships, change, creativity, science, deepening spirituality and for the greater good.

Pisces

Great timing for magical workings concerning dreams, completion, increasing psychic ability and intuition, flow. Also a good time to do healing work around women's cycles.

Aries

Great timing for magical workings concerning stamina, leadership, dealing with authority figures, strength, study.

Taurus

Excellent for magic concerning family and children, love, home matters, purchase of real estate, creating sacred space in the home.

Gemini

Great timing for magic concerning expansion, communication of all kinds, travel, writing, invocations.

Cancer

Great timing for magical workings concerning all kinds of emotional healing, cutting cords of old relationships. Great for healing the body, promoting health particularly through diet.

Leo

Excellent for magical workings for self-esteem, personal power, status, authority of all kinds, improving your relationship with your boss.

Virgo

Great timing for workings concerning getting or keeping a job, exams, purification, clearing, detoxing of all kinds.

Libra

Excellent timing for magical workings concerning balance, justice, all legal matters, better health, weight loss.

Scorpio

Great timing for magical workings concerning all sexual matters, healing trauma, reducing gossip, increasing fun.

Sagittarius

Excellent timing for magical workings concerning truth, exposing dishonesty, clarity, and to ask for increased travel or protection during travel.

THE MAGIC
STARTS HERE

Thre are three vital skills to learn to get started with lunar magic. This is how I begin with my students who are serious about working with earth elements and lunar energies, and for all of them, you need nothing but yourself.

It is tempting to get all kinds of tools and fancy goodies to connect in with magic. Yes, those crystals are beautiful. That wand is wow, something else! But YOU are the weaver of magic and magic starts with you. That is more than enough.

Here is the first skill.

Observation

Allow me to suggest that for a whole lunar cycle, 28 moons, you get a real life visual for each moon. You do this by going outside for just 5 minutes and observing the moon. If the weather is inclement or for some other reason you can't go outside to get a visual, that is alright, you can look at the moon through your window or car window.

The key here is to *observe.*

To really actively notice what the moon is doing and how it might be different from the previous night.

You'll notice, too, the stars and planets around the moon. If it is cloudy you'll notice the way the clouds form and disappear around the moon. You might notice, if the conditions are right, a luminous circle around the moon, or even small rainbows emanating from it.

Look, too, at the surface of the moon. Can you see any patterns or details? What colour is it? What are the textures you can see?

And finally check in with yourself. Observe how you are feeling whilst watching this moon. What emotions or thoughts are flowing through your mind and body?

By doing this and this alone for a moon cycle, you will automatically become much more aware and sensitive to both how the moon affects you and how the moon's energy and appearance changes during waxing and waning.

The second skill is:

Sitting Out – Utiseta

The ancient Norse had a complex spiritual and religious system that was very much based in nature. The elemental character of their lands – fire, ice, snow, extreme weather, volcanoes, steam – shaped not just their creation mythos but also the way they connected with their deities. For example, the first man and woman, Ash and Embla, were created by Odin from trees.

The whole Norse cosmos of nine worlds was cradled and nourished by wyrd of the great world tree Yggdrasil. The moon was a god, Mani. The underworld was ruled by the goddess Hel (not to be confused with the Christian concept of Hell), and all kinds of animals ran across the branches and pathways of the tree bringing magic and messages.

There were landvaettir, which were nature spirits or sprites. Similar to the idea of '*genus loci*' in Latin. For the Norse, they are found near rivers, streams, wells, forests and mountains. They don't shapeshift but they can appear as anything therefore one had to be aware of one's surroundings so they were not offended or hurt.

The idea of being connected with nature was something almost automatic for the Norse, a civilisation who were incredible travellers and navigators and paid close attention to the directions and the movements of the sun and moon, stars and tides.

The practice of purposeful 'sitting out', called utiseta (oot-e-setta) was a meditative and somewhat shamanic activity. Utiseta meant you spent time, generally overnight, meditating and sleeping on the land with the moon above, allowing the land and sky to connect and speak with you. The trance magic practitioners called seidrkonas and the volvas (witches) often slept on their blue capes directly on the burial mounds of wise folk who had passed and would share their visions with the village in the high hall the next day. However mostly, utiseta was, and still is, a technique also used for far sight, meditation, contacting dis (protective energies) and landvaettir, and for decision making.

Now, you might say this is a very fancy way of talking about sitting on the ground under the moon. Well, yes, you would be right in some aspects! However, how many of us place our backs upon the earth and sleep anymore? How many of us allow our hearts to actually touch the mother earth or open like a blossom facing the moon and stars? We just don't see this as an important activity anymore – unless you are someone who has fallen in love with camping or sitting outside for long periods.

What does utiseta do that is so important?

It links us with our essential essence as a human animal, part of a wider ecosystem. It connects us deeply to the rhythms of the light and dark, moon and sun, the moon phases, even the energies present where you are – whether or not you actually believe in them. We get to quiet ourselves, reject any drama and chaos and envelop ourselves in our ancestral right of being a part of the universe under that big moon. This is awe inspiring and confidence building.

Am I asking you to utiseta every night? No. Most of us live in the city and this is often hard to do. I would encourage you, for starters, to try and either sit or lay out in your garden if you have one for three or more hours for one night each lunar cycle. Maybe if you get comfy doing this, you could try a sleepover (be safe of course) or go camping. Even once a year under a full moon is a fantastic way to start.

Remember utiseta is purposeful. When you do it, make an effort to connect with the elements – the earth and the moon. Maybe take a recorded guided meditation or learn one that is second nature to your mind. Open a circle, get moon-baked, and eat and drink something you like.

Enjoy.

The third skill:

Casting Circles

When I was learning about paganism and the craft, one of the first and simplest lessons in magic I was taught was how to cast a circle. The creation of a circle is the creation of sacred space within which you will perform processes that are markedly different from anything else you do in your 'normal' world. In lunar magic, it is a reflection of the shape of that big moon above you and is a way to capture the energy.

The idea of casting a circle is a very ancient one and it is to ready, steady and focus the mind on the magic that you are going to perform. Its protective nature gives the mind and body notice that you are safe and will not be disturbed. By marking this new space, it signals to the mind that you are travelling to another realm where everything and anything is possible. *It is a signal to the subconscious to pay attention.* Stepping into your circle is stepping into another world and another state of mind.

To me it is the easiest way to change my state into something powerful and positive.

Traditionally, in some witchcraft traditions, circles are opened by 'cutting' the fabric of time with a special double-bladed knife called an athame. Athames are only used ceremonially and are never used to cut anything else. Athames are sacred tools and each athame is used only by its owner. However, if I often find myself somewhere where the use of an athame is inappropriate, like a public place, there are many other ways to create your sacred space.

There is no singular way to cast a circle, although most traditions open and close their circles in a particular way. Circles are usually opened counterclockwise and closed clockwise in the southern hemisphere (the opposite stands for the northern hemisphere). This follows the sunrise direction or deosil. At the beginning of many spells, there is a call to cast your circle. At the end, there will be a request to close your circle. To open a circle, call in each direction from their position in the circle. (You may need a compass or the compass on your phone to know this accurately). Here are some preferred ways of casting circles:

Use the athame and cut the fabric of time to create a sacred circle.

Walk a circle barefoot.

Throw flower petals on the ground in the shape of a circle.

Stand in the middle of the circle and trace it in the air or ground with a pointed finger.

Sprinkle sea salt around the edge of your circle to mark the boundaries.

Place small votive candles around the circumference of the circle.

Trace a circle with your finger into the soil or sand around where you are standing. Mark the circle with a sweep of a wand, feather, or special crystal.

A simple prayer or invocation is usually spoken as you trace the circle. An example is:

"I open this circle. I ask that only good enter and that I am protected. As above, so below."

And when you close the circle:

"I close this circle. I leave it blessed and protected. As above, so below."

Or:

Opening: "Under the protection of the moon, the stars and the earth I step forward and open this circle where magic happens." (step counterclockwise)
Closing: "I am grateful for the help of the moon, the stars and the earth as I close this circle where all I have woven stands true." (step clockwise)

You are free to use these simple invocations or to create your own. But what you say is up to you as long as it creates a boundary of 'otherness'.

Advanced practitioners will normally engage in some energy raising to extend the boundaries of the circle or to send energy flowing fully around the circle if there is a group ritual.

One of the jobs of the priestess is to raise, hold and send energy especially in group situations. This kind of control takes time and expertise to learn and develop. It is akin to walking into a gym for the first time and expecting to lift the heaviest weights straight away. You have to train and condition yourself to work with bigger volumes of energy.

A good way to start this process of raising energy within your circle is by connecting to the earth, pulling energy upwards and holding it within yourself then eventually doing the same thing but sending it outwards as well as connecting to other energies and elements like the moon.

This process is an ancient one and is common to many pagan cultures.

It can go like this:

Stand outside, barefoot if you can. Feet hip width apart.

Take a big deep breath in and out. Exhale any anxiety or worries you may have at that moment. Take your time.

Place your awareness in your feet. Close your eyes.

Feel the earth under the soles of your feet. Take a breath and extend your energy down into the earth beyond your feet.

Take another deep breath and upon the exhale send your energy further into the earth.

Inhale the energy of the earth. Take your time.

Feel the earth's warmth and the way it is alive. Allow your energy to extend sideways too, like the roots of a mighty tree. You are so secure and grounded right now that if someone tried to push you over, they couldn't.

When you feel ready, take a big breath in and pull up that earth energy. Pull it up to your feet. Just your feet.

This energy will give you a sensation in your feet or body. Invite this energy to you.

See it.

Hear it.

Smell it.

Taste it.

FEEL IT!

Pull it up now to your ankles, knees, thighs, genitals, swirl it around your hips and belly. Keep breathing. Allow it to come up your spine. Now into your heart where it travels through your veins and arteries to everywhere! Breathe and pull it up, right to the top of your head.

Hold it. Allow your body to absorb what it needs.

Put your arms out to the sides and when you are ready, send some energy out through your hands. Imagine yourself as a conduit, a connection – allowing the flow of energy that is your birthright to charge through you.

At this point, advanced practitioners may send this energy to the rest of the circle (group ritual) or they may open themselves (crown chakra) further to the lunar or divine energies, with a kind of 'meeting in the middle' experience. Earth and moon or earth and divine (higher power) energies are meeting within you. Again, this is not for beginners and should be something that is built up to with a good teacher.

When the point you wish to reach has been achieved, you reverse the energy, allowing it to fall back to the earth, always giving a little of ourselves in gratitude and reciprocity.

REAL MAGIC AND
HOW IT WORKS

Spell Craft

When I began my first tentative steps into witchcraft, one thing that bothered me was just 'how did it all work?' How could I trust something to help solve my problems or direct me to something better when I didn't have a firm understanding of what or how 'it does it'? How did this thing called magic direct things so that the world swung my way? I consider myself very much a creative person but also very rational, so I really needed to sink my intellectual fangs into something other than what seemed at the time lots of mist and smoky curls.

Real magic does have a scientific basis. With quantum physics now putting forward firm theories around some of the ancient principles such as 'we are all connected', and that 'we can influence our own reality', more and more previously disinterested people are going to be leaning towards discovering more about metaphysical solutions such as the ones featured in this book.

For me though, knowing the miracle of how this works enhances and strengthens the magic and it allows me to be able to share its secrets with you. That way, you can learn how to replicate it and weave it for yourself.

The Logic of Magic

Our mind has conscious and unconscious levels and this is a scientific fact. Much of our learning occurs in our unconscious. It is also the place where our dreams, our creativity, our desires, and our motivations develop. Spells and rituals bypass the conscious part of the mind; much like hypnosis and trance does, and sends messages to the deeper unconscious. The unconscious then takes these messages and hones in on what you want without you even being aware of it. In other words, what you clearly focus on, especially in your deep unconscious, is what you will work towards and manifest.

The unconscious speaks a language quite different than the conscious. The unconscious loves metaphors, colours, symbols, movement, archetypes, prayer and storytelling. This is the language of rituals and spells. To be able to get the most out of this language, there are five elements – the grammatical rules if you like. These elements enable you to reach the power of your unconscious most effectively.

The Five Elements

Strictly speaking, most practising witches observe a variety of different rituals and have a good knowledge of spell craft. What I will present here is the backbone or core elements that make up the anatomy of a spell or ritual. It is important to note they are not specific to a particular tradition. For those of you who are already following a path, feel free to integrate your practices where you see fit.

I always say when I am teaching spell craft that if you can construct a spell to the five elements I am just about to give you, you can always write a good solid spell. If there is one thing I want people to be able to do, it is to be able to go away and do this themselves! This is a valuable skill.

Most spell crafts and rituals are constructed with the same five elements. The way you express these basic elements is always unique and completely up to your creativeness.

These are:

1. FOCUS
2. PURPOSE and INTENTION
3. RAISING POWER
4. RELEASE
5. GROUNDING and PARTICIPATION

Depending upon the purpose of the spell or ritual, energy raising and grounding may or may not be necessary.

1. Focus

You know that what you put your attention on manifests. We are what we *do.* So then, every action that you take towards making what you want clearer and more focused will bring it closer. In practice, there are certain methods to focus your efforts and intentions.

The first focused step might be to create sacred space for yourself. You can create a sacred area by casting a circle and perhaps arranging an altar in a significant way. You might decide to burn some incense or herbs.

However, for those of you new to this work, any preparation for the spell, even if it is making a list of the items necessary and then going shopping for them, helps focus your mind on the purpose and intention of the spell. By focusing, you tell the unconscious that something different is about to occur and to pay attention.

2. Purpose and Intention

Magic needs direction. Energy also needs direction to be effective and powerful. To do this you need to clearly define and state the reason you wish to perform the magic and what you intend to do with the energy. Without this clarity you are never focused enough to reach your goal or desire.

Feel free to write down your purpose and intention. Do make it short and to the point. No essays here. To be effective, your purpose and intention should be a summary of what you want and why you want it. I will also suggest that although you need to be concise and confident, do not get so detailed that there is little chance for the energy to get really creative.

I will give you a simple example. Let's say you wanted a new house. In a spell, you would not ask for a house that was on a particular street, was white, had a picket fence, green grass, two bedrooms and a view of apple trees. Instead, what you would ask for is a house that has all the attributes that you are looking for. You would ask for a house that is beautiful, safe, has a garden you love, in a convenient and lovely location, and spacious enough to accommodate all your needs. You may get your house with the picket fence and green grass. You may not... but what you will get is what you have asked for. This, of course, will be perhaps more than you could have described in detail. You are allowing a co-creation. You will not be disappointed.

Never intend things for others unless you have their permission. This is breaking the law of 'Harm None'. If you wish to cast a spell on behalf of anyone or include anyone, even if you think it is for their best interest, ask permission first.

These are some of the questions I pose to my clients when they come to me for a spell. As you will see, these questions encourage the client to focus their mind on what it is they really intend.

What would I like to achieve by performing a spell? Summarise into two or three concise points.

What would a good result look like to me?

What do I see as the greatest obstacles to achieving my intention at the moment?

What is the urgency of this matter to me?

Am I willing to do my spell outdoors, perhaps in a public place, or would I prefer to keep it completely private?

Do I have any particular beliefs around spells or rituals that I believe will help or hinder the process?

3. Raising Power

Even the space shuttle needs a rocket engine to get it into space. Raising natural power is even more powerful than any engineered engine in flinging forth your desire into the universe. Raising power is the truly magical element of a spell. You will know when you begin to raise power correctly. There is a physical change. You will always feel it. The physical attributes are different for everyone. You may feel the hairs rise on the back of your neck, you may feel energised, or suddenly feel serene. It is common to feel your hands tingle, your breath pattern change, and to notice your heart beating and that your posture is powerful. The physical attributes are different for everyone, but when raising power you will always feel a surge in emotion.

It has been said that emotions are e-motions: energy in action. This is evident when raising power. Whatever emotional state you were in at the beginning of the spell that emotional state will change when raising power. It may be amplified or change all together.

4. Release and Grounding

You construct spells in such a way that the energy of energy is raised so that it propels forward the purpose and intention you have. When the energy is at its peak you will feel an irresistible urge to release it... to fling it forth. There will be a moment in raising power that you feel like letting it all out. This is when the unconscious will really sit up and notice that you are serious about this intention. This is usually the point in your spell when you release to the goddess what it is that you are asking for. It is the climax of the spell. Depending upon the spell or ritual, you may be chanting, blowing out a candle, breaking a bowl, tying a knot, dancing, burning something. In sex magic, it is the point of orgasm which does the release. Whatever it is, you will receive a signal that you are releasing your intention to its destination powered by the energy that you have raised.

After you go through the previous three stages and have then released the power you raised, you may feel like you are still carrying excess energy. This can manifest in a feeling of being hyperactive and buzzing. Or, in contrast, you may feel tired and drained. This may develop into a serene, calm feeling or an unpleasant fuzzy feeling. You need to find a way to change the mood and energy flow of the magical plane and return to this reality. This process is referred to as grounding.

Witches traditionally grounded themselves by having something to eat and drink, known as the 'cakes and ale' of the old texts. Witches also chose to ground themselves by uniting with their partner in climactic sex or by masturbation. This enabled them to get back in the body with the bonus of pleasure thrown in. Another traditional grounding technique is to place your hands palms down onto the earth and send the excess energy back to the earth and the goddess. I love this technique because it improves my garden.

Many modern witches choose to ground themselves by having a glass of wine, listening to music as they dance round the living room, meditating, running or even doing gym work. Whatever way you choose, the key action here is to rid yourself of that extra raised energy and to stop generating any more by changing your state as quickly as you can.

5. Participation

Now it's your turn to go out into the world and make things happen. You are co-creating with the goddess now so start moving. The goddess co-creates; she doesn't just give, which is magical thinking as I told you about earlier. The spell or ritual you have performed contains your focus and intention and it will be propelled out into the universe but very little will happen if you are not travelling along to accept what you have asked for. We need to be reminded to step up to be able to receive the better life we have asked for. If you go out into your world and begin to actively participate and move towards what your purpose and intention are, and with the confidence that higher forces are working with you, I have no doubt you will experience a higher rate of success.

Otherwise it's just smoke and mirrors, isn't it? It is just us playing around.

Start small if you like. But start. An analogy I like to use is taking that first step is like tipping over the first domino of a long line. Once that first one falls, there is a knock-on effect of consequences with all the others. You will start a chain reaction of events that will lead you towards what you desire.

And record your progress in your Book of Shadows. I cannot emphasise how important this is. You will soon see how what you have focused on is coming to fruition and this only adds to your momentum.

THINGS TO
REMEMBER

Privacy

Yes, if you are casting alone, it is important to situate yourself somewhere where you are unlikely to be disturbed and I understand for some of you this may be a problem. But I also know humans are ingenious creatures. If you want some privacy you will find it. I have cast in airplane toilets (no candles of course), in my car (no smoke), cradled in a tree branch (no dancing) and in a friend's garage (roller door down). Again, plan your spells ahead of time and you can plan your privacy more effectively.

Let me also say this about privacy; it is not the end of the world if you are interrupted. It will not take anything away from the end result as long as you aren't too rattled.

Just do what I do: smile broadly and ask, "Can I help you?" If they are not on fire or dying, I then tell them I will be with them in thirty minutes or so and make it clear that the conversation is over for now. I have not once had someone press the issue. You can explain what you were doing later to them when you are ready, if you wish. If you have kids, that may be harder, so unless you wish to include them, doing your spell work after they are in bed may just be what you have to do.

Never Interfere with Free Will

There is this really strange misunderstanding about witchcraft, spells and rituals, and it is that the whole system is for controlling people. Nothing could be further from the truth.

The image of a witch or shaman casting a spell or curse to control the actions of her 'victims' is still a potent one today. In the past, witches were often accused of controlling the minds of their victims, and in the 'burning times', it was easy not to choose to take the responsibility for one's actions and to simply blame a witch for 'making you do it'. Witches (and independent women in general) were scapegoated for lots of things that had absolutely nothing to do with them. Those accused who made confessions would often blame the devil (yes, the devil made me do it!), which is also a breach of their own free will and a surrender of personal responsibility.

The idea that witches commonly cast love spells for their clients to ensure that someone falls in love with them is something I deal with almost every day. By asking a witch to assist you to make someone love you or fall in love with you again is impacting the target's free will. It also breaches our central tenet of Harm None. I will have no part in this kind of spell casting and neither will any other ethical practitioner. I suggest that you don't either no matter how tempted you may be.

One of the central guidelines of many pagan witchcraft paths is the idea of Harm None, and by interfering with someone's free will, I would be changing the natural way of things and enforcing my will over theirs.

For example, take the love spell – no matter how desperate the case, I will never cast, or assist anyone to cast, a love spell that involves a specific 'target'. Instead, I will ask the person to refocus their intention on what they want, list the attributes of the ideal partner they wish to attract, and cast for that, not a person they know. That way, no free will is being affected. If the person my client desires is in fact the person that the universe sees as ideal for them, the person will be attracted. Wonderful! If not, there will be someone more suitable who will enter the scene. A win/win situation!

Always check that the spell you are casting or the ritual you are performing does not interfere with someone else's sovereignty. A little check someone suggested to me once was to ask myself: "Would I like that someone is doing this ritual involving me without my consent?" Almost always, the answer is no.

Personally, I even ask people's permission to send them healing energy before I do, and by people, I even mean my family and close friends – such is my dedication to the respectfulness of free will. If someone is very sick in hospital and, say, cannot give permission, I do the healing work but add a kind of insurance policy of "... if this be for their highest good and they wish to receive this..."

Go with the Flow...

Magic is a wonderfully organic and personal thing. Energy raising is individual and I am making suggested guidelines to stick to in a spell or ritual, nothing more. Do not feel as though you need to control every element of the ritual.

Letting your power mingle with the spell is what makes the magic absolutely yours. Again, YOU are the magic, you are a conduit.

You know now that spells have a clear, proven anatomy that makes them work. If you stick to that strong skeleton, the detailed fleshing out can be as unique as you are. So be in tune with the deeper parts of yourself and with the goddess or higher energy when you are spell casting. If you instinctively feel like changing a part of the spell as you are performing it, change it. You will KNOW when to stop chanting, you will KNOW when your power is at its height.

Feel like laughing? Do it.

Like crying? Do it.

Feel like getting up and dancing around? Please do!

Which leads me to the subject of HAVING FUN!

We have all become quite serious beings. We are busy, we have deadlines, we have schedules, there are difficult relationships, little time, burnout. There is a lot that can get in the way of a peaceful mind and a few good belly laughs. Certainly be mindful of what you are asking for, and be respectful of the all-powerful energies that you are dealing with, but this does not mean you need to be overly heavy and serious all the time. Doing this work has always been a celebratory way of life and its joyous nature is certainly a balm to the overworked soul.

Let your mind and body have fun. This is one of the key reasons spell craft and, in particular, lunar-based magic works. You are bypassing your conscious self and targeting your unconscious which has a sweet love affair with symbols, music, colours, rhyming, trances, intentions and FUN. Whether performing a spell alone or with a group, the fastest way to feel connection is to allow some fun into the proceedings. In fact, it has been my experience that those spells that I have had the most fun creating or the most pleasure in performing have given me the fastest results.

A GUIDE TO LUNAR RITUALS

Drawing Down the Moon

One of the most famous lunar-based rituals practised by witches or priestesses is that of drawing down the moon. Whilst the current incantation of this ritual is part of many Wiccan traditions, other traditions and cultures like the Norse Seidr and Artemistic temple workings have similar ritual processes.

Each full moon I often choose to celebrate by performing this ritual, that of drawing down the moon. I will either do a simple version typically involving a reflective bowl and athame, where the moon reflects in the water of the bowl and the reflection 'drawn' down either anoints one's body or one drinks it, or I will take part in a larger ritual of trance magic.

Drawing down the moon has, at its heart, trance magic. It is the epitome of being moon struck!

Trance magic is an extremely ancient kind of magic that involves changing one's state of consciousness, usually so one can receive messages or visions from the Divine. It is induced by ritual, meditation, drumming/music, dancing or substances (e.g. plant medicines) or a combination of all.

In this case, trance is induced in the priestess by the moving reflection of the moonlight directly into her eyes and by the structure of the ritual itself including chanting. Each coven or temple has its way of doing this and it is one of the mysteries of that group. The priestess is trained over time to be able to undertake this work safely and in some cases she takes on the energy of a divine being within her body. This is the kind of advanced magic that should be taught and assisted by experienced practitioners who know how to teach this and to create a safe psychological and physical environment.

A gentle way of engaging in this style of ritual for the beginner is to open your circle, connect with the earth's energy (draw attention to your feet first), and ensure you pull up that energy solidly and hold it flowfully in your body.

Then, look up and connect with the moon. Do this with soft eyes. Allow your vision to stare and become unfocused after a while. Allow that moonlight to flow through you from the top down.

Keep softly focused on that moon. Breathe.

If you are doing this correctly, letting go under the moon, you will 'lose time'. This is when your unconscious mind takes over – trance. This is when you are accessing that huge and wise and wild place of your unconscious. This is useful to do if you are stuck and can't move forward or cannot work creatively through a problem. I have had many an idea for my writing this way and also I find my mind goes almost straight into a kind of journey somewhere – and these have been the basis of a number of the guided meditations I write.

The other thing to try is to draw down the moon with a partner and a bowl of water and a small mirror.

Open a circle which you'll both stand in. Face your partner. Your partner has the mirror. You are holding up the bowl of water. Have your partner point the mirror at an angle to the moon so the light reflects downwards into the bowl. You will see the moonlight rippling in the bowl of water and it will dance. Keep your eyes and focus soft and follow the dance of the moonlight on the water. You are drawing down the moon to yourself! Allow the feeling of this to flow through you.

Notice how you feel. Enjoy.

Then swap around.

You can also do this solo, by holding the bowl of water yourself and angling so that it catches the moons reflection and its light dances in the bowl. You then imbibe some of the 'aqua luna' (moon water) just as though you were drinking moonlight.

Solo Ceremony/Ritual

If you are going to work with the moon, you will most likely wish to do ritual or 'ceremony'. In fact, everyone right now seems to be running around doing things that sometimes aren't really rituals at all, but some beautiful looking tableau for Instagram.

Firstly, what is a ritual?

A ritual is a specific order of activities often weaving actions, words symbology or objects, performed in a special place and according to a previously set sequence. It has a clear purpose.

For example, cleaning your teeth every morning and before bed is a kind of ritual. Your purpose is to clean your teeth and have oral hygiene. You have a set sequence of actions, at a set time using a toothbrush that is yours, toothpaste and water.

A ceremony has a ritual within it. A wedding ceremony, for example, has a rite or ritual of marriage within its whole. It is something larger that encases a ritual.

For the purposes of this work, I won't be making a huge distinction between these terms other than I think it is more important to get you doing purposeful lunar rituals regularly, and then you can, if you wish, create wider ceremonies around them. The Wheel of the Year rituals lend themselves to greater ceremony.

Again, there is a structure to a good ritual and it is similar to spell craft in that there should be:

1. FOCUS
2. PURPOSE AND INTENTION
3. A WAY OF RAISING POWER TO CHANGE STATE
4. A CULMINATION OF, OR RELEASE OF, POWER
5. GROUNDING AND PARTICIPATION

Firstly, we should decide what we wish to achieve in the ritual. It could be simply a devotional one, sending love and gratitude to our patroness deity or to the divine energies. It could be that it is for a purpose such as gratitude, for more prosperity, for love, better health or relationships.

This helps us focus on what we need for the ritual and how we prepare.

A ritual should always have an 'action' about it – otherwise it is a meditation. For example, we might consume something or burn something in a ritual. To imagine doing so, rather than actually doing so, indicates a meditation rather than a ritual.

We raise power (energy) to help the intention get out into the universe and we do that in an almost infinite variety of ways – from music like drumming, to physical action, to elemental engagement, to voice work, and once we are at the pinnacle of that we release our purpose and intention outwards with power. How we release is again up to our creativity, but it should be markedly different than the way we raise energy.

For example, I could get the energy raised and flowing by dancing but I would not dance to release it. I could suddenly be still and use my voice to send it out, or I could leap over something and stop.

This is, of course, experiential (you have to do it, to know it) so if you are a bit puzzled by what I am saying, please do some rituals in this book and you'll soon get the hang of what I'm saying.

The ritual should then be grounded in some way – in the old days that was usually by eating or drinking something (cakes and ale) and this is to bring us psychologically and physically back to our bodies.

Finally, if the ritual was to help us achieve something, we should agree to take some steps towards what we have asked for. This is especially important if we are working with a deity and have promised or vowed we will do our part in manifesting what we have asked their help with.

Why not try these few moon-based rituals to start with?

Moonrise Ritual

This is a ritual to welcome the full moon. You can perform this simple ritual each full moonrise.

I take note of the time of moonrise or I go somewhere where I can actually see the moonrise from the horizon.

I gather a white or silver candle and some fragrant oil for anointing myself.

I open a circle.

As the moon begins to rise, I light the candle and say:

"Behold the moon, the light of which runs in my veins,
I welcome you."
"I stand under this moon, as my human ancestors did
Feet upon the earth, head raised, heart open.
Thank you for your blessing tonight."

I bow my head to the moon.

I then place a drop of oil on my wrists, the top of my head and my heart.

I watch the moonrise if I can.

I am grateful.

Close the circle.

New Moon Fresh Start Ritual

This ritual should be performed on a new moon. Alternatively, on the waxing cycle. You can perform this alone or with others, and it needs to be done outdoors with access to the earth. Wear something pretty and place flowers in your hair!

Gather an egg, pens or textas to write on the egg, fresh flower petals, a variety of seeds suitable for your garden or the place you are casting, a flask of water, a small spade or large spoon to dig a small hole and a small green candle.

Ahead of time, write some wishes and good intentions on your egg. For example, you might write simple words or symbols representing what you would most desire with a fresh start e.g. growth, peace, more love, creativity.

Create a circle of flower petals and step inside with joy. Light your candle and say:

> *"Oh! I honour this new moon! I ask for the blessings of the gods and goddesses in my quest for rejuvenation and fresh starts!"*

Now take in the energies of this moon, the feeling of the air on your skin, the smells of the evening. Be aware of the birds, the sound of the trees in the breeze. Look around you: absorb the colours of the night sky, the ground, the flowers. Take a deep breath.

Now hold the egg in your hand and charge it with all these good vibrations and feelings. Feel the energy flow from the earth to your feet to your body through to your hands and the egg itself.

Make a small hole in the earth now.

Then say:

> *"A gift for you, Great Mother! Thank you for all you do for me."*

Crack the egg you have been giving all that great energy to into the soil. If there are a few of you, step out of the circle and all crack your eggs in different places.

Now sprinkle the seeds around the circle, expressing your gratitude.

Blow the candle out (safely).

Dark Moon Release Ritual

This is a great ritual to do at the end of each season to release any residual unwanted energy and, of course, during dark moon. By completing a ritual like this, it enables us to move forward into the growth aspect of the year with less burden and more lightness.

Firstly, take some time alone and write down on paper anything that you would prefer to leave behind in this cycle. For example, this may be a belief or fear that you no longer wish to entertain or even a habit you wish to release. The more searching and honest you are, the better. Then, when you feel you have a complete list, go outside to the garden (or if you don't have a garden, go to a park) with a candle and a small spade. Find a spot near some trees or healthy plants.

Light the candle and say out loud:

> *"Universe, I ask that you assist me to leave behind these things I no longer need so I can move forward in growth and positive momentum."*

Then read out your list and notice how it makes you feel. (Hint: It shouldn't make you feel good!)

Next, think about what it would be like NOT to have these things in your life anymore. This should make you feel good! Enthusiastically, tear up the list and, using your spade, dig a hole and put the pieces of list in the earth. (An alternative to burying them is burning them in a flameproof bowl, but only do this at home.)

Know that the universe will now take those negative energies and recycle them for good. You will already feel freer and know that the process has already begun to create a happier, lighter, better you! Blow out the candle with thanks.

Importantly, write down one action that you will take towards this brilliant new start and away from the old 'you'. Ensure you participate and do what you say you will.

Large Group Ceremonies/Rituals

Lunar-loving ancestors would often make their ceremonies a village or regional thing. This would mean big groups. On the popular Wheel of the Year festivals like Mid-Summer or Beltaine in Europe, we know people travelled for days to sacred sites and literally thousands of people joined in the celebrations.

With group ritual, we have many people gathering for the same purpose, raising power together, creating. So how is organising group ritual different than solo?

Well, I decided to gather solid information for you from someone who runs large public rituals on a regular basis. David Garland is the founder and president of the Pagan Awareness Network (PAN), which is the largest pagan educational organisation in the southern hemisphere. David and PAN have a southern hemisphere record of over 22 years of unbroken organisation of a public full moon circle. That's right, every full moon, David and his team run a ritual under the full moon in Sydney.

Having been to a number of these circles, the great thing about them is their welcoming nature (often these are the public's first experience with a witches/pagan circle), and how the circles encourage involvement, yet are very organised. They are also very safe places to be and you feel like you are in good hands when you go.

When I asked David for his advice on running large circles (especially in public), his first piece of advice was to make sure you have all your local government and/or police permits. This ensures you stick to the rules of the local area or public space and gives you guidelines of what you can and cannot do.

David told a story on this matter, about how the first circle was picketed and demonstrated against by a group of christians and it all got a bit heated and the police were called. David and PAN were the ones with the public permit, and so just on that point, the loud demonstrators were told to move on and some were arrested.

The second point David made was about inclusiveness in that everyone should be made to feel as comfortable as possible and that the organisers are organised! This means not just what happens in the circle but what happens outside the circle... for example, first aid, security, who brings the food (if any), what is your contingency plan if someone just rocks up and interrupts or starts to ask questions etc.

His third point was to ensure everyone knew that if they were uncomfortable in any way, it is okay to step out or just watch this time. Setting up a cocoon of psychological safety is paramount. Sometimes people feel strange or uncomfortable raising power for the first time. I personally felt empowered the first time I felt the rush of a lot of energy in group ritual, but this can also trigger a fear response in some people. As organisers and ethical practitioners, we need to know this ahead of time and let folks know that if they wish to step away, this is totally alright. Respecting people's sovereignty and free will is very important in magic.

Here is an Outline of the PAN Full Moon Circle

This is a traditional witchcraft/Wiccan style format which has been altered a little so it creates a circle catering for everyone whether completely new or advanced.

Hosts get there early and bring all ritual items with them.

People start to arrive.

The host will be there to welcome participants and may offer simple roles to those who wish to have a more active part in the ritual.

The host will gather everyone and go through a quick rundown of the ritual and talk about any other pertinent information they might need.

Participants enter the ritual area and the area is ritually cleansed.

The circle is cast.

The quarters are called (the guardians of the 4 directions and 4 elements are invoked).

The goddess and god are welcomed.

A meditation and a ritual working will be performed. This may take the form of chanting, dancing, group spell work or wolf howl. (PAN are famous for the wolf howl which is a fun way of getting everyone involved in raising and releasing energy.)

'Cakes and ale' are blessed and shared amongst the group. (Not literally cakes and ale, although it can be, but this is the old term for sharing food together.)

The quarters, the goddess and the god are farewelled.

The circle is closed and the ritual completed.

Announcements are made and people chat and ask any questions they may have. (This is a fantastic, safe place to learn.)

Hosts stay and clean up any rubbish or signs that they were there.

EVERY MOON IS A MAGICAL MOON

I want to say this very clearly: EVERY moon is magical. EVERY moon.

Yes, the new moons and the full moons get all the glory and attention but magnificent lunar magic is available to you on every moon.

Witches and other pagan people have been working with the cycles for a VERY long time. Most of us use all the cycle if we need to or want to. One of the most common pieces of feedback I get on my 'Queen of the Moon' oracle deck – which breaks down each moon phase into themes, suggested magic and meaning – is the delight of those new to this kind of alchemic magic that it's not 'just about the full moon'.

I have been teaching about and creating spell craft around the use of natural cycles for decades now and if there is one thing I would love people to understand around the lunar cycle, it is this.

Forgive me if I sound a bit exasperated when I speak about this, but I just see the current trend of folk only hitting up the full moon or the new moon as a magical time for spells or rituals a lot. When this time comes around you see all these memes on social media about the particular new or full moon and you rarely see anything at any other time. So in this book, I decided to make sure you understood that every moon is a magical moon and that you can cast upon any moon you like.

Now are there more optimum times to cast magic for specific intentions? Yes. Absolutely. However, I believe that cycles are useful and they teach us to be flowful and inventive with our workings. It is a cycle after all and one with no beginning or ending.

THE
28 MOONS

As I have mentioned, *every* moon is a magical moon. Every phase is worth our attention.

Every moon is an opportunity.

Every moon can have the weaving of our magic happen, and this is a conveniently great thing. Why? Because life happens and we cannot always wait for what is considered the most super-duper auspicious time.

I have always cast when I have most needed it, and yes, sometimes that means I can wait, but sometimes due to the complexity of life, I cannot. At the latter time I have looked at the moon phase and I have adjusted my spell to best suit that time.

We are all busy people and waiting for ten minutes and three seconds past 2 pm on a Sagittarius full moon, which may be two months away, maybe, just maybe, isn't going to work time-wise for you. And frankly, what I'm going to reveal to you, even though it certainly isn't what most practitioners who want you to rely on them for advice on perfect timing want you to know, is that it doesn't matter that you are not nailing exact timing; what matters is that you have your intentions clear and strong and your power raised.

There are always multiple ways (or lunar strategies) to get what you want.

For example, let us say, I want better health. I can go about this a variety of ways with the moon cycle.

I can cast a spell on the waning cycle to remove the barriers to vital good health. I could also cast on the waning cycle a spell to reduce any disease or pain I have.

On the dark moon, I could ask for healing and balance and pull in the assistance of a dark goddess or god to assist me, like Hekate.

On the new moon, I could ask for a fresh new start for my body and for it to renew and the cells to heal faster.

Since we are in the waxing cycle, I could use that to build energy and power towards healing and coping better, by building courage and confidence to blow away any fears I may have.

Then we are at full power at full moon and I can ask for anything I like.

So as you can see, basically you have 28 moons (or all or any part of that cycle) to do effective workings for yourself.

This is the witches' way – practical and magical.

Following is a profile on each moon and the emotional, magical and physical themes of each. I have given a little more time to the big three: dark, new and full moon because these are key pivot points in the cycle.

I have added a spell, ritual, invocation or meditation to each so you can get a feel for the phase's opportunity. All are authentic, tried and tested workings and I hope you enjoy and benefit from them.

Think always of this as a cycle, each moon infinitely connected to the next, like a fine web. This is a guide, it should not limit your own exploration and creativity.

Dark Moon

Themes:

REST, RELEASE AND RESET. THE VOID AS A TIME OF POSSIBILITY. LETTING GO OF THE OLD AND CRUSTY. THE CEASING OF RESISTANCE. SURRENDER IN A POSITIVE WAY.

There is nothing to fear in letting go of old negative patterns and habits.

Whilst full moon gets all the publicity, dark moon is just as powerful in its own way. Whilst full moon means full attractive power, dark moon offers the infinite possibilities of a clean slate.

In some cultures, the dark moon and the way it appears – it often looks like just a darker piece of the night sky – harkens back to the idea of 'the void'. A place of unknowable secrets, a state of 'everything and nothing' or a place to prepare or rest before moving on. To me personally, there is a restful quality about this darkest of moon that allows pondering and decisions about what we can jettison before making plans for the moon day.

Know that this moon is powerful, but it is incredibly gentle too in the way it helps you unravel what isn't working, so you can embrace a fresh start.

If you find yourself resisting the dark moon, it is usually a sign that you are being fearful and stubborn about letting go of something that is old and is no longer serving you in a positive way. Often that is an old fear or pattern that was created to protect you in some way, however now it is outdated, yet you are still carrying it or acting it out.

Relax, reframe and think about how much better your life will be without that bad habit, fear or pattern. Get very clear about the possibilities of this transformation and what it will give you in real terms. This is the power of the dark moon; it allows you the most optimum time in the cycle to release the old and cut the cords of relationships and traumas that deserve no time and attention in your present.

Cutting the Cords Ritual

Cutting the cords must only be undertaken when you are indeed ready to move on to a different kind of relationship or different aspect of life. If you are cutting the cords with a person, this by no means indicates that this person will be cut out of your life completely (although this may in fact happen). What it will mean is the part of the relationship that no longer serves you will be cut and will disappear. Nothing negative from that time forward will bind you to this individual.

This process creates change that is far reaching and highly beneficial, however it normally has emotional processes such as grief attached to it, which, normally, is not considered a pleasant or desired state. States such as this however are a natural and necessary part of healing and moving on, better than before.

You'll need:

- A glass of wine or moon water to open the ritual
- White candle to represent the goddess and a red or black candle to burn through the cord if you choose to burn through. A small sharp knife for cutting the cord if you choose to cut rather than burn
- Cord long enough to go around your waist with enough room to fit your fist between your waist and the cord. Choose the cord size that feels most right for you. I favour silver or gold cords
- Personal item from the relationship that you are willing to get rid of
- Bowl in which to place the cord after it is cut
- Tongs for picking up the cord after it is cut
- Lighter to burn cord after cutting
- Small spade for burying the cord and personal item
- Comfortable robe to put on after the ritual if you are doing the ritual skyclad
- Your support person, if need be, who can facilitate you through the ritual

Open a circle in whatever manner you choose.

Light your 2 candles with intent.

Take a sip of wine or moon water.

Ask for your patron goddess and possibly a goddess of purification such as Sekhmet to be present. Offer them something they may like on your altar. (Sekhmet loves red, beer or even a statue of a lion.)

Make sure the room is warm and comfortable. Disrobe if you are doing the ritual skyclad.

State what it is that you are here to do.

For example:

> *"Goddess, I am here before you tonight to cut the cords with XXX. I wish to transform the relationship I have with them into something that serves me. I ask for your help and protection tonight."*

Now lay down or kneel down. Relax. Breathe in the power of the universe. Begin to imagine yourself floating in darkness. It is very quiet. It is very beautiful. You are not afraid, nor are you alone completely, as the goddess(es) are there with you. Look around if you choose and see them in whatever form they may take.

Look around you. Notice the many points of light that have appeared. Almost like stars. Move closer towards them and you will realise that these light points are becoming people you know. Past and present.

Search now for the person that you wish to cut the cords with. When you find them, open your eyes and tie your cord around your waist, leaving it loose, so that it is not big enough to step out of, but big enough at least to put your fist under. Leave room enough that you can cut it or burn it easily and safely.

Close your eyes and sit upright or better still stand up firmly... do not lie down. This is a time for action.

Think about, in sensual detail (touch, taste, vision, aural, feeling), your interactions with this person. Do not dwell on the good or romantic bits if these are what come to mind first. Be slightly detached around these as if we are still feeling pain in these areas. It is very easy to romanticise or enlarge these as 'bigger' experiences than those that are more unpleasant. Similarly, if you are only thinking of the 'bad' experiences, become slightly detached.

When you believe you are feeling what it is to be connected to this person with all your senses, imagine them in front of you. Look at them... all of them, not just their eyes or face. See them in 3D in space. Spin them around if need be so you take in all of them.

Now imagine that there are fine cords linking you to them... they can be as they are, so do not edit how they look. Sometimes they appear like fine spider webs, sometimes like thick cords, sometimes plaited and perfect, sometimes rough or fleshy. Notice this and look at the detail and importantly notice whereabouts you are joined on your bodies and how.

You may feel sensations at the location of the cords. If you are afraid or worried here, ask for your facilitator's help or for your patron goddesses to be closer.

Decide now whether you will cut or burn through the cords... it is up to you.

Now imagine that you have a sacred knife or scissors or flame in your hand. It is now time to sever/burn the cords that bind you. (This does not mean that you will not see the person, love them or feel any other emotion. It just means that the nature of the relationship you now have with them will be severed. It will end or transform into something new.)

In your mind or out loud, thank the person you will be cutting the cords with for the lessons that they offered and taught you. It is now time to let this relationship, in its current form, go.

Ask for your goddesses to protect you and to be with you.

In real life now, open your eyes, hold the cord in one hand, and your cutting/ burning implement in the other.

State plainly and strongly:

> *"I wish to cut the cords with XXXX. I want the old connection that does not serve me to be severed/burned away, and for me to be free and renewed."*

Now again recall the person and the relationship in its detail. When you are ready, CUT THE CORDS. Say:

> *"I cut the cords that bind me! I let you go with love and honour!"*

Breathe deeply, feel the cords drop from your body (in real life and in the metaphysical world). Close your eyes and watch as those cords that connected you earlier have fallen or do fall away. If there are any left, cut them in your mind or ask that your patron goddess assists you with the cutting. Take your time with this. Ensure you cut or burn them all.

Now breathe again deeply and relax. Close your circle.

All is new and will be better. Be supported if necessary. Allow yourself to feel what you feel.

Ritual of Grounding and Protection

Open a circle if you wish. Stand strongly in the warrior pose (feet firm on the ground and shoulder width apart, knees slightly bent, back straight. Arms slightly away from the body, hands may face up or down).

Breathe deeply. Imagine now that your feet are connecting with the earth like roots in a tree. With each breath, receive the goddess-given power from the earth knowing that this power is unlimited and protective.

If you like, you could imagine that this power has a colour and a texture and it is running up your body like an electric current or a slow-moving vapour (whatever you prefer). It is permeating every cell, renewing and protecting you.

If you have a patron goddess or god, now is the time to call upon them for extra protection and to be with you.

Now state where you need and want protection. Feel your energy rise. Feel you have what you need.

When you have all you need say:

| *"I feel your protection and love, I am shielded!"*

Close your circle. Give thanks.

New Moon

Themes:
Beginnings and fresh starts. Having the courage to take your first steps. Health and wellbeing. Sexual healing. True renewal. Beginner's mind.

There is something incredibly poetic and even romantic about that tiny sliver of silver that is the new moon. After the waning cycle and the depth of dark moon, here is, appearing incredibly in the sky, a crescent of the finest light. Almost a scratch upon the blackboard of the universe, here is the evidence that even after the darkest night, light returns again.

When the new moon appears in the lunar cycle, we are gifted with a new beginning and a fresh start. What we have identified as useless or unneeded any more has been released in the void of the dark moon and here, awaiting, is a new chance. Yes! Here we get to renew our lives and feel free enough to risk trying again.

Whether you are asking for a fresh start in relationships or a new love, or you are heralding the actioning of intentions such as better health, a new business or the start of a new project, riding the new moon energy assists us. Many creative people start new works on a new moon and I personally, as an author, like to begin all my new works on this phase, even if 'beginning' means typing up a cover page or outline. The most powerful of new moons traditionally are within the spring season.

Sexual Healing Ritual with the Goddess Freyja

You'll need:

- A gift for Freyja
- White feather
- Piece of amber or gold. For example: amber incense

Have your intention about how you wish to feel clearly in mind or written down and where you need most of Freyja's healing. For example: I have been hurt by partners in the past and feel afraid to invite someone new in.

Gather:

- White or gold candle
- Gift for Freyja
- A bottle of your favourite perfume
- Symbol of your new confident sexual self... a stone or piece of gold jewellery
- Paper and pen

Cast and open a circle if you wish.

Light the candle and say out loud:

> *"Great Goddess Freyja, you who are mighty and beautiful,*
> *You who are wise and lovely*
> *I wish to feel your essence and I wish to be healed."*

Leave the present for Freyja near the candle.

Imagine Freya as you would visualise her, or feel her, in front of you. Take your time. There is no right or wrong way.

Take several deep breaths. Imagine being the person you wish to be – fully healed, confident, sensual, loving in an openhearted and strong way. See, hear and accept what it would be like. However it is for you, imagine these attributes flowing and being breathed into your body. The feeling should be extremely pleasant. Hold the symbol in your hand and allow this new energy to imbibe it.

Say:

> *"Freyja, Goddess of Love, Sex and Magic – help me now. Tonight is the*
> *beginning of something incredibly important. Tonight I will raise my power*
> *of attraction and my love of self. Tonight I accept complete healing for myself*
> *in your name."*

Now be aware of how this healing in her name makes you feel in your body. This should feel very good. Feel it warm you, pulse through you.

Now spray the fragrance upon the new you!

Breathe in deeply. As you breathe in, you are inhaling even more attractive power. Freyja is with you.

Thank Freyja.

If you opened a circle, now close your circle.

Take the energised symbol (now a talisman) with you. Note how different you feel and act upon this!

Waxing Crescent 1

Themes:

WITH SELF-AWARENESS COMES REALISATION OF WHO WE ARE. TRUTH. KNOWLEDGE. SELF-EXAMINATION AND PERSONAL RESPONSIBILITY. UNDERSTANDING YOUR ROLE IN THINGS. EXAMINATION OF 'WHAT IS'.

As we move into the early waxing cycle, light begins to shine upon the shadows, illuminating what is. This is the beginning of a powerful process: realisation. When we decide to really examine our lives without fear or favour, it can be difficult. This is, no doubt, an act of profound courage. We might not like what we discover after all. Yet without self-awareness and the will to act upon those realisations, (whether we perceive them as negative or positive) we do not get to change and grow.

The realisation that we have a pattern, a bad habit or a behaviour that is causing us pain is a powerful position, even though we may feel worry and pain around this discovery. We can then take personal responsibility to change our position since we know our current position. Knowing ourselves more completely enables us to accept ourselves more readily and to dare to love exactly who we really are.

Welcoming the Light Invocation (with the God Apollo)

Invocation:

This is a wonderful invocation to this powerful god who brings light and foresight to situations. He is also a god of music so make sure you play some music.

You'll need:

- ❍ A golden candle
- ❍ Some incense or burn a bay leaf
- ❍ Your favourite music playing or if you play an instrument even better!

Light the candle.
Put the music on or play some.
Then say:

> *"Lord of the Light, Archer of Life*
> *Light Bringer,*
> *I thank you for your light of truth.*
> *I embrace my present. I am grateful for everything in my life.*
> *Every day gets better,*
> *As I become more self-aware of who I am and what I want.*
> *Every day brings more illumination to my life."*

Now close your eyes and imagine a golden light surrounding your body and breathe this in and out. Imagine it travelling through the heart and the blood and the cells of your body – lighting up every single part.

Now speak one word out loud – a single intention – that you would love to manifest for this time. Offer this feeling/intention to Apollo.

Open your eyes.
Thank Apollo
Blow out the candle.

Waxing Crescent 2

Themes:

ACCEPTANCE OF WHERE WE ARE IN THIS POINT IN OUR JOURNEY. THE POWER OF 'RIGHT NOW'. ACCEPTANCE IS THE FIRST STEP TO CHANGING ANYTHING. SELF-EXAMINATION AND THE AWARENESS OF DUTY OR RESPONSIBILITY. MAKING OUR HOME A SANCTUARY FOR OURSELVES.

All of us at some time have dodged our blind spots and had the illumination of 'what actually is' confront us. What we do next is crucial. Do we accept exactly where we are, no matter how painful or confronting? Or do we retreat back into our illusions?

Choosing to accept ourselves fully and the position we are in enables us to take that next step towards growth. When we can plant our feet solidly into the earth and say, "Yes, here is exactly where I am and I accept this fully", then we can take the next steps confidently, honestly and powerfully towards where we now wish to head. Accepting where we are right now in its fullness allows us to also accept that there may be some chaos in our change before there is full order again. This can be an exciting feeling rather than one that generates fear if we hold our new intentions clearly.

Making our home as we wish it to be is also part of this acceptance of where we are. If it isn't a place of absolute sanctuary for us it is hard to feel we are secure and grounded.

Blessing for your Home

Centre yourself and call upon the friendly fires of Vesta to bless your family and your home. If there is conflict within your home, she can assist. If there is a member away from home, due to travel or work, she can offer her protection.

You'll need:

- ◯ A large candle in gold or flame colours like red. Ensure that it can be safely left burning for some time
- ◯ Sand to be used to draw a circle
- ◯ Incense
- ◯ Flameproof bowl
- ◯ Fresh flowers

Ahead of time, think about what you would like to wish for positively for your family and home. You might want protection, joy, happiness, prosperity and good health, for example. Write this down on a piece of paper.

Prepare the flowers in a pretty vase and place on the area you are doing this blessing. Then trace a circle on the sand and place the candle in the centre.

Light the candle and say:

"Blessings upon you, Lady Vesta
The very centre of Rome
She who is the protectress of home
She of the centre of the earth
She who protects all around the holy hearth."

Now read your list and tell Vesta what it is that you might wish. Do this out loud.

Now take a deep breath. Imagine having all of these things for your home and family, allow this positive emotion to rise. Take your time.

Read the paper again and then say:

"I release these requests to you, Vesta, and know that they will be granted."

Burn the paper over the flame. Pop it in the bowl so you don't burn yourself. Thank Vesta for her help and burn the incense.

Allow the candle to burn for at least a few hours in her honour.

Waxing Crescent 3

Themes:

SEEKING ACTIVE GROWTH AND CHANGE. REJECTING STAGNANCY. MOVING FORWARD TO GET UNSTUCK, TAKE ACTION. CHOOSING THE HIGHER SELF NOT THE LOWER PATH.

The waxing lunar cycle calls for growth but not growth without aim or purpose. When we understand our current position, accept it and decide to change, we will naturally grow as people.

We might experience some 'growing pains', after all transformation of any kind is rarely completely easy and trouble-free, yet if we go where we wish to grow then isn't it worth it?

Having a strong intention of what the results of our growth will be helps with gaining the courage to move forward with our growth and into the eventual blossoming of our true self.

Ritual of Growth

You'll need to be outside for this spell. Be barefoot.

Take a deep breath and place your awareness into your feet for a moment. Imagine that they are extending the earth a little, like the roots of a tree. Continue to breathe and extend your energy down in a grounded way.

Now when you have done that, bring your awareness to your skin. Feel the moon's light upon your skin. Feel how pleasant that feels. Feel the power of this. Know you are doing what millions have done before you.

Say out loud looking up at the moon:

> *"Hail and welcome*
> *Loving circle of all*
> *You who bless with light and strength*
> *Bless me now with the power that is my birthright."*

Breathe in and as you do imagine you are breathing in the moonlight. Allowing this glowing light to enter your body.

Imagine this light that is life giving, permeating and lighting up every single cell. EVERY SINGLE CELL!

Keep breathing and taking in this energy. Allow anything that does not serve you to simply leave your body. You need not try to do this, just allow it – there is simply no room for anything that is a burden, stuck or heavy.

Say:

> *"I feel your power! I take what is offered! Thank you!"*

Continue to charge up as long as you like.

Give thanks.

Waxing Crescent 4

Themes:

BEING YOUR OWN CHEER SQUAD. DEVELOPING RADICAL SELF-LOVE. EMPOWERMENT STARTS FROM THE INSIDE OUT. FOCUSING ON YOU. NOT COMPARING YOURSELF TO OTHERS.

Sometimes we feel we are not enough. Sometimes we are even told we are not enough by our own voice, the voices of others and our culture. Not smart enough. Not pretty enough. Not powerful enough. Not talented enough. Not good enough at what we choose to do.

Or maybe that we are 'too much'. Too tall, too short, too fat or too thin. Too wrinkly, pimply, too old, too young. Too quiet or too mouthy. Too noticeable. Too opinionated. And all this makes us not love ourselves enough.

Know that this comparison craziness is just a diversion to knowing yourself really well and discovering amazing, delicious aspects of yourself that are entirely satisfying. Focus on you, not others and discover where you really might like change, if anywhere or anything, for your own personal benefit, not for some outward measure of 'enoughness'.

Here is the moon that says: Please just stop. Put your blinkers on. Breathe. Be with yourself. Do ritual. Speak to the goddess (or whatever energy floats your boat) and ask for help to fall in love with yourself again.

This is one of my favourite spells for self-love. It features the Greek goddess Aphrodite.

Loving Yourself with Aphrodite

You'll need:

- ◐ Fresh flowers (roses are lovely)
- ◐ Shells, apples or small mirrors (optional for your altar)
- ◐ A hand mirror
- ◐ A white candle
- ◐ A small amount of rose, rose geranium or olive oil

Lay some fresh flowers on your altar. You might add a shell or a mirror that are symbols that would be pleasing to Aphrodite. Light the candle and say:

> *"I call you, mighty Aphrodite, Goddess of Love. I ask that you bless me with love all around me, but first with a love of myself."*

Now hold the mirror so you can see your face. If this is too difficult, hold the mirror towards your heart. And repeat this invocation once every new moon until really seeing yourself is comfortable.

> *"Allow me to see my own beauty, even though I may not at first feel beautiful.*
> *Allow me to experience my own true love of self, even though it is easier to love others.*
> *Mirror back to me my worth as I sometimes struggle to recognise it.*
> *Help me see I am a goddess,*
> *As I come from a spark of you."*

Think about where you would like healing around self-love and state this strongly. For example: "Great Aphrodite, oh gold-crowned queen of love and beauty, I need healing around... (state here your situation) and how I have been hurt in the past. I ask that you see me and heal me."

Feel the blessings of Aphrodite fall upon you and anoint your wrists and forehead with a little of the fragrant oil.

Blow out the candle with thanks.

Waxing Crescent 5

Themes:

CHOOSING TO NOURISH YOUR MIND, BODY AND SPIRIT. FEED YOUR VALUES AND STAND BY THEM. WHEN WE ARE JEALOUS OR WE ENVY, IT IS A SIGN AS TO WHAT WE ARE ACTUALLY HUNGERING FOR. PAY ATTENTION TO YOUR HEALTH.

All of us have a set of values that are as individual as our fingerprint. Sometimes we aren't sure what they might be if asked, but unconsciously we know. How do we know? Because if our values are not being met or lived, we rebel. We get angry, sad, depressed, irritable, stuck or we take the chaotic choice in our decision-making and commonly our relationships and life is not harmonious.

We get hungry for the life we want to live. Meeting our values and living through them is a sure way to nourish our being. We feel more complete and fulfilled.

Learning to nourish our bodies purely to give them what they really need is a key to mental and physical health. Do not allow food to become a diversion or pain relief rather than something that is nourishing, health bringing or even simply enjoyable.

Ritual for Health and Vitality

This is a beautiful ritual to perform for one moon cycle (28 days) to improve your health, self-love and vitality. It is perfect to do after your daily bath or shower and should only take you an extra 5 minutes in your schedule.

You'll need:

- Some fragrant massage oil or your favourite body cream. Try something aromatherapy-based if possible
- Handful of coarse rock salt

During your bath or shower on day 1, take the rock salt and rub it with a little oil over your body from top to toes. As you lightly scrub the salt over your body, ask that any barriers to your good health and vitality be removed. If you know of a particular existing health problem you may have, imagine that problem being washed away by the salt and your body cleansed.

Towel off lightly and, beginning with your toes, begin to massage the oil in. As you massage each part of your body, say something positive about it. For example: "I love my toes because they keep my feet balanced, I love my feet as they take me everywhere I want to go, I love my ankles as they are slender, etc." Most of us do have a part or two of our bodies that perhaps we don't love so much. It is very important to find something great to say about these parts in particular. Don't forget to mention organs such as the heart, kidneys and stomach.

When you get to the top of your head, chant three times:

"I love my body and mind,
Health and vitality are mine,
I ask that blocks be removed,
Bless me, Goddess Divine!"

Now get on with your day knowing that you are developing radiant health and vitality! Repeat for the next 27 days for best results.

 ## Waxing Crescent 6

Themes:

Keep moving, keep progressing. Being confident – the way is open for you and the path is illuminated. Begin the journey now.

When we accept where we are, acknowledge what needs to change to grow and begin to love ourselves more completely, the direction of our lives starts to change. We often decide we want to follow a more authentic way for ourselves, and our desires become more aligned with the needs, wants and values of our true selves.

Imagine that we are lost in a dark forest and we can hardly see. There is no visible path and every way looks exactly the same. We feel burdened by shadows. We are not sure that we should even move because we are so paralysed by fear and uncertainty.

Then, the sunshine somehow breaks through the clouds and the leaf canopy and there ahead is a path, illuminated in golden light. It is clear now, the direction we should head. The path is not only visible but it is inviting us forward and so, instead of just standing there, we can't wait to step upon it and move forward.

Invocation for Increased Inspiration Featuring the Goddess Brigid

You'll need:

- Spring flowers
- 2 small white tealight candles
- 1 large candle preferably orange or red
- A small piece of worked metal (jewellery is good)

Light the big candle saying:

> *"Great Bride, Great Brigid, Great Brigit, I call but a few of your names. Beloved of the smiths, the bards, the scholars, I ask for your fire to warm me from the inside out!"*

Light one small candle. Tell Brigid honestly about your project or how you are feeling about your life as it is. For example: "Right now, I feel passionless about my work situation. I feel like I am in a rut..." or "I have this XYZ creative project that I am trying to get off the ground and I'm not confident I can do it...!"

Then hold the worked metal and say:

> *"You who create from fire, help me create from it too! Let me burn with passion, grow hot from inspiration, let me forge the work that I want!"*

Then light the last candle.

> *"This is my future – burning bright!*
> *I thank you, Brigid, knowing that you will be lighting my way and that inspiration has begun!"*

Allow the two small candles to burn down. Then blow out the big candle with thanks.

Ask Brigid to give you great ideas ongoing.

Keep the metal with you when you work.

First Quarter Moon

Themes:

ASSESSMENT OF YOUR CURRENT POSITION. GETTING CRYSTAL CLEAR. WE MUST MAKE SURE OUR BLIND SPOTS ARE REVEALED AND THAT WE ARE HONEST WITH OTHERS AND OURSELVES.

You have begun your journey and now it is time to assess where you are and what to do next. You have decided, you have worked and walked the path for some time and yet, you understand that in every journey, it's a wise action to check the map!

Now is the time to look carefully at all aspects of your life and especially the areas in which you have set some intentions or goals. Ask yourself: Do I still want these things? Do I still want that same end result? (And if the answer is 'no', what can I do to not lose momentum, pivot and head towards what I now desire?)

Assessing, although seemingly not a glamorous act or term, has a high payoff for us if we bother to do it well. Doing it well means we really look, and look hard at how things are going. All of us have some kind of blind spot so it's worth exposing this by consulting a trusted friend or seeing where negative repeating patterns are and looking for the cause. Shining a light on a blind spot and taking action to shift it is one of life's big catalysts for change.

Waxing Gibbous 1

Themes:

TAKING TIME TO DISCERN CAREFULLY. JUDGING WISELY. THERE MAY HAVE BEEN SOMETHING DIFFICULT TO SEE, SOMETHING THAT HAS BEEN OBSCURED, BUT NOW IT HAS BEEN REVEALED TO YOU.

Hopefully the time you spend moving and choosing upon this earth brings you some kind of wisdom. Or at least some of that wisdom bred of hindsight and perspective. Instead of taking things on face value or rushing into surface judgements, taking your sweet time to form friendships and business relationships; putting your energy output into proper scale and busting some nasty patterns if they are there hiding in the corners.

All of us, if we are engaged in life, make good decisions and poor ones. Sometimes we make spectacularly bad ones. All of us get hurt, hurt others, learn, forget, fall over, fall over again, get up... but hopefully, we GROW. We change. We are able to spot where our sore points are and fix them if we so choose.

The secret here is discernment. REAL discernment. Really making it a priority to take time to ensure acuteness of judgement. Sort of really looking at the 'fine print' before you buy! This is true wisdom developing.

This is the first of the Waxing Gibbous Moons. The overall themes of this part of the moon cycle are action and will.

Deep Ice Scrying

This activity can be started at any time but is most powerful on a dark moon or waning part of the moon cycle. Seeing visions in a reflective surface like ice is described as ice scrying. People of the northern hemisphere use ice scrying as just one tool of divination, but you don't need natural ice to try it yourself. A freezer will do!

You'll need:
- A small tea light candle
- A pan or tray for ice

A biscuit or shallow bake pan is perfect. Fill it with the purest water you can find. The purer the water the clearer the ice. Distilled or spring water is perfect, inexpensive and available in most supermarkets. Then pop in the freezer until completely frozen.

Pull out your ice tray or plate. Allow it to warm just a little by pouring a tiny bit of water on the top so that the ice crystals on the top melt and the ice surface is wet and clear. Then, light your candle and dim or turn off all other light sources.

As with any kind of scrying, the enemy of effective ice scrying is distraction... both from inside and out, so turn off your phone and try to have a quiet environment.

Settle your mind. If you regularly meditate you may wish to use those techniques or I find simply shutting my eyes and focusing on slowing my breathing is effective. If I have a specific question for the ice, I state it now.

Once I feel relaxed I open my eyes but turn my focus inwards. I imagine pulling my energy within me and then I focus on the third eye point (the chakra point on the centre of the forehead just above the eyebrows) and I imagine opening it.

At this point, I may wish to call upon or invoke a goddess or god to assist me. Ice or winter deities are ideal here. Why not ask for the help of the Inuit Goddess Sedna, Skadi the Norse Goddess of Winter and the Hunt (The Ice Queen from the Norse Pantheon), or Hod, the blind Norse god of darkness and winter.

Now, again relax and gaze into the surface of the ice. Focus on nothing but it. Soften your gaze. You will notice that the light changes on the surface as the candle glows and flutters. Look deeper now than the surface. Notice that there is no end to the ice, that there is just an infinite space. Allow messages and images to form.

Let go. Allow.

When you have experienced your divination journey, write down anything that seems important.

Give thanks and blow out the candle.

Waxing Gibbous 2

Themes:

THE TIME FOR COURAGE IS HERE. FEAR IS ONLY USEFUL IF IT IS TEACHING YOU SOMETHING. YOU MUST EXAMINE WHETHER YOUR FEARS ARE OLD OR NEW, USEFUL OR UNHELPFUL. FEAR BLOCKS FLOW. THE TIME FOR COURAGE IS HERE.

This is a great moon for fear busting and hey, don't we all get scared about something sometimes. If there is one thing that stops people from fulfilling their dreams – or even getting things done that they want done – it is fear. Whilst having fear is built in and a part of the way our brain works to protect us, it is chemical (yes, emotions like fear are chemical and they send off a whole raft of body chemicals to give us the best chance of coping with situations that need our attention to survive).

There is a healthy kind of fear. The kind that warns us to keep out of a dangerous situation or stay clear of someone who instinctively repels us. However, it would be a rare person who does not have at least one fear that does not serve them. A fear that is unrealistic, untrue, perhaps based on an outmoded experience or something that is buried so deeply that we only see the symptoms rather than the fear itself. Most fears have been formed with a positive intent of protection. We need to separate that intention and deal with it in a more resourceful and less destructive way if we are to create ease and flow in our lives.

Fear has many names. Some covert like envy, jealousy, co-dependence, procrastination, bullying, people pleasing, disconnection and some more overt like fear of failure or fear of success.

There is, however, a kind of antidote to fear and it is courage. Fear will put up an initial resistance to courage but it has no real long-term power against it. It is worth developing.

Being Fearless Invocation with Kali

Give your fears to one of the most powerful dark goddesses of all.

You'll need:

- ◯ A red candle
- ◯ A small amount of ash placed on a small plate (you can make this by burning some wood, fragrant sandalwood chips or some charcoal and resin)
- ◯ Incense

- ◐   Pen and paper
- ◐   A gift for Kali

Light the candle saying:

> *"Great Mother Kali, I call upon you to help me to reduce and destroy my fears. You who kills demons. You who are fearless! Bless me and protect me."*

Now out loud describe the fears you have, what is in the way, what these fears cause you to do. Use specific examples and be honest even though it may be hard to talk about. Know that Kali listens and is responding.

Say:

> *"Kali, I seek a better and brighter life, yet my fears hold me back. They bring me into darkness. Some of them are big. Some of them are hiding. You who are change itself, you who defeats the shadow in me, from now, show me how to move forward fearlessly. What do I do next to facilitate my change into being more fearless, Great Mother Kali?"*

Write down any ideas/messages you may receive on the paper. (You will action these later.)

Now place your index finger in the ash and then anoint your forehead with the ash (third eye position in between eyebrows).

Say:

> *"Kali, thank you for my blessing. I agree to participate and do my part. Thank you!"*

Leave your gift on your altar or space.

Waxing Gibbous 3

Themes:

LEARN HOW TO SAY NO AS A COMPLETE SENTENCE. JUDGING WHAT YOU NEED AND WHAT YOU DON'T ALLOWS YOU TO PLACE HEALTHY BOUNDARIES. WE TEACH PEOPLE HOW TO TREAT US. JUDGE WHAT IS HEALTHY AND RIGHT FOR YOU WITH CLARITY AND CARE. SIMPLIFY.

In times of sickness or the presence of very strong emotions such as grief, we often naturally simplify. We cut out all the 'extras' that are too hard or too complex to do at that time. We might not take up an invitation to an event that we might have to 'work at' being at. We might only want to see or communicate with friends we know and trust understand us and love and support us, warts and all.

Now, what if we did this all the time? What if we consciously chose more simply and specifically for the benefit of our own mind, body and spirit? Yes, life is complex but it can be richer and more enjoyable if we pare back what is 'negatively extra' and choose a more deliberate and authentic path.

This moon is also powerful for actions towards righteous action and justice. At some point in our lives, justice may not be done externally or immediately.

Spell for Justice

You'll need:

- A feather (white preferably)
- Set of scales or two rocks the same size
- Your legal or justice issue written down
- Flameproof bowl
- White candle

Light the candle and say:

> *"Maat, Goddess of All order,*
> *Queen of Justice,*
> *Fair weigher of souls, I ask for your assistance in resolving a legal issue."*

Hold the feather over your heart and say:

> *"You who will grant justice, if it be for the highest good of all, grant me*
> *success and resolution around this issue..." (and tell Maat about the issue and*
> *where and how you want justice).*

Now place the feather on one side of the scales or on one of the rocks. Say:

> *"I believe my heart is light and I ask that I recognise my part in this..." (tell*
> *Maat about your part in this, no matter how small).*

Now take the paper and hold it over the candle, burning it. Say:

> *"I leave this judgement in your hands, Great Maat, knowing that your justice*
> *is swift."*

Relax in the knowledge that natural order will be returned.

Take the feather outside and release it to the wind where it will be received by Maat.

Blow out the candle.

Waxing Gibbous 4

Themes:

EMPHASIS ON THE DRIVE OF OUR PERSONAL WILL TO MANIFEST WHAT WE WANT. DECISIONS REQUIRE ACTION. I AM IN CONTROL OVER MY OWN DECISIONS AND LIFE, NO ONE ELSE'S. PASSION AND WILL DETERMINE A GREAT PROPORTION OF SUCCESS. I WILL PERSIST.

'Will' seems like a very old-fashioned concept. In our modern world where it seems like everything is geared up to be as easy as possible or there is always someone else to blame, the idea of placing our personal will persistently into something seems quaint.

When we decide we are going to change something in our lives, let's say particularly a negative pattern or bad habit, breaking the old way we do things can be difficult. The change requires a concentration of our will. We may want the change, but it is our will that will insist that we stay on the path to that change. To be wilful means that we have the power of control over our own actions and that will fires up the persistence that we need to get what we want.

In witchcraft traditions, contrary to popular belief, practitioners do not interfere with another's free will. This means we do not cast spells upon people or do a casting to influence their behaviour.

How do we get what we want instead? We cast on ourselves in line with our will, focusing carefully on what we would like in our lives instead. To use our will well, we should have assessed what we really want and be sure that this is what we want to reach for.

Spell for Money and Prosperity

Think about exactly what you need the money or increasing your prosperity for. Is it for bills, your mortgage, for the kids' school fees or for travel? If it's just to improve your general flow of prosperity concentrate on that. You can do this spell indoors or out.

You'll need:

- Some gold coins and some banknotes. Overseas currency is just fine
- A small purse or drawstring bag. A small jewellery pouch or bonbonniere bag is fine
- A green or gold candle
- Some dried basil from your kitchen

Take a deep breath and sprinkle the basil around you in a clockwise circle. Light your candle saying:

"I humbly ask tonight for greater flow of prosperity to me and more money to improve my life."

Stand up, take a deep breath and imagine your feet are like the roots of a tree, delving deep into the abundant earth.

Taking the bank notes and coins in the palms of your hands, imagine that the incredible power of the abundant earth is entering your feet, running up your legs# [insert space]and body, and then allow it to enter your hands and the money. Now speak out loud what it is you want the money for. For example: "I need money to pay off the mortgage, bring it to me!" or "I require money for a long-awaited trip to Thailand, let it come to me quickly!"

Now, imagine what it would feel like to have that money. Allow your emotions to be felt, and at the peak of that experience say:

"This money will be my talisman to attract more!"

Place one coin in your wallet or purse. Place the rest of the money into the drawstring bag, and place under your pillow for the next 28 days.

Blow out your candle and sprinkle more basil but in an anticlockwise motion.

Waxing Gibbous 5

Theme:

FOCUS ON THE TASK AT HAND RIGHT NOW. PUT ON THE BLINKERS AND DO NOT LISTEN TO GOSSIP OR NEGATIVE PEOPLE. CHOOSE YOUR FRIENDS WISELY. IF YOU MAKE A MISTAKE, IT IS YOUR MISTAKE TO MAKE. DO NOT SPLIT YOUR ATTENTION TOO BROADLY.

This moon teaches us that what we place our focused attention on matters. Placing our undivided focus on something means we are more likely to take action upon it. We are more likely to finish something we wish to complete if we focus on it. We are more likely to plan and succeed in our achievements should we take the time to focus on how.

What hinders focus? Diversion. And often it is diversions we set for ourselves or that we allow. When we are afraid of our own growth or greatness we may procrastinate. We might place drama in our own way. We may even focus on everyone except for ourselves and, of course, never have the time for the things we set for ourselves. Our heart's desires never come to us.

Perhaps instead we allow others' opinion of us to get in the way. We allow the criticisms and values of others to affect us. Forget about what others think of you or gossip about you or even what society says. Seek true friends, not those who would destroy your peace and focus.

Focus instead on what feels so deeply good to you, what you really want and what you want to place your laser-like focus upon. And soon, it will be yours.

Ritual for True Friendship

There are few joys greater in life than having true friends. Whilst every friendship has its tests, many of us would be very happy to have around us people for whom loyalty, love, support and laughter are part and parcel of the relationship you have with them. Mithras is a wonderful deity to call upon to ask for new friends, to strengthen or repair friendships and even to ask for fairness in relationships.

Light a candle and say:

"Great Bull of the Stars, you who was born from the earth's womb
I call thee.
Mithras, star of Perseus, strong and wise, you who need no tomb
I petition thee
Mithras of the moon and sun, you who have no end, you who sacrifice for others,
I ask thee: (state your issue and your intention around friendship)
I make my pledge here and now to be the kind of friend that I would like to have.
In your presence
For balance, for fairness, for honour, for action, for loyalty and love
For the greatest good of all,
Ave, Mithras!"

Now shake your own hand in a bond. Take action towards your intention.

If you like you may leave a small offering for Mithras such as a picture of a bull, or drawing or a rock.

Be very aware of how friends act over the next moon cycle and act accordingly.

Waxing Gibbous 6

Themes:

BEING RESPONSIVE. THE TIME HAS COME TO TAKE ACTION. LET GO OF YOUR PARALYSIS. LET GO OF YOUR BURDEN. STEP BY STEP AND DO NOT STOP. CREATE AND EXPAND!

It is natural sometimes to be afraid to move forward. Maybe we have failed before. Change can be difficult if we have been hurt before and so we are anxious about what may happen if we have another go. Maybe we think it's easier and safer to just tread some water for a while.

Instead of taking joyful action towards the things we truly desire – say the writing of a book, undertaking study, accepting a new job, seeking a better relationship – we baulk, we freeze, we do not take the steps we could. And so we remain stagnant. We don't grow.

This moon phase encourages us to embrace action. Action is part of our humanity. We are not made to hide and refuse to blossom. We are here to expand and be fertile in all ways.

Ritual for Creativity and Growth with the Gaelic Goddess Danu

This is a powerful spell to assist you to plug into the creative power of the earth itself and flood yourself with the fertile creativity of Danu.

You will need to do this spell in nature. Day or night is suitable. Perform the spell barefoot. Place flowers in your hair.

You'll need:

- Flowers for your hair
- Jug of water
- Seeds to plant

Stand up straight, put awareness into your feet, breathe in and pull up the energy of the planet. Take your time.

Now take a deep breath in and on the out breath place your awareness in your feet – specifically where your feet are in contact with the ground. Close your eyes, take another breath in and on the out breath extend your energy past your feet into the earth. Hold in your mind and body this feeling of connection with the earth.

Feel the Mother Earth begin to connect with you. Every breath enables you to go deeper, wider, more expansively into the earth itself. When you feel very connected – and do take your time – say:

> *"Danu, Great Mother of the Earth,*
> *Of the laws of nature, of the cycles of life, of the Tuatha Dé Danann,*
> *I ask you to extend your magic to me.*
> *Connect me to who I am and allow me to grow and create in your name."*

Now think about where exactly you might want creativity, in growth or with a flow of fertility. Feel what it would feel like to have/be/experience this situation in its fullness. Feel now the power of Danu's blessing and her love as she floods you with creative power from the earth.

Feel it in every cell! Take your time. When you feel it, open your eyes, and claim it and say:

> *"Danu! I feel your power and I accept your magic and your gifts. Help me be worthy and to remember I have power and it is real."*

Now pour the jug of water upon the ground and plant your seeds.

Thank Danu and take one real life step towards your creative intention as soon as possible.

Full Moon

Themes:

YOU HAVE POWER. IT IS REAL. STEP INTO YOUR TRUE POWER. SHINE BRIGHTLY. DO NOT HIDE WHO AND WHAT YOU ARE. THE TIME IS RIGHT TO ATTRACT BIG THINGS FOR YOURSELF. ANCESTRAL ENERGY IS IMPORTANT. OPEN YOUR MIND TO BIGGER POSSIBILITIES. BIG POWER, BIG MAGIC.

The full moon reminds us the world has magic and we are a powerful part of this force. Full moons give us awe, wonder, the feeling that the world is a miracle and that we can weave our own.

From the time humans could perceive a moon, we used it for our spiritual uses and full moon triggers the same feelings in us countless millennia later. This is the moon of Diana, the one Aradia danced under, the fleeting light in the dark forest that lights the way for Artemis, the embodiment of the Norse God Mani, who guided the ships on the sea. This is the moon that our human ancestors have marvelled under, prayed under, made love under.

The full moon reminds us to think big, to shine our light brightly and to know that we indeed deserve to have our big dreams come forth. It is a moon that you can cast on for almost anything, the power being so huge, so just give thanks and go for it.

Often before doing ritual on full moon we take a ritual bath. Here is a suggestion:

This recipe is made up in a larger amount so you can share with your friends. You need a handful for a beautiful spring bath that is not only revitalising but magical!

Ahead of time you'll need:

- 500 grams of good quality coarse sea salt. I like the Himalayan salt because of its rosy colour and properties but there are many other kinds
- 500 grams of Epsom salts or magnesium salts
- 100 grams of dried lavender
- 100 grams dried rose petals or rose buds
- 50 grams of dried calendula petals
- 50 grams of dried mint
- Large mixing bowl
- 10 drops of lavender oil
- 10 drops rose geranium oil
- 5 drops jasmine oil
- 5 drops bergamot oil
- 5 drops cedarwood

Place all dry ingredients in the bowl and as you stir them all together with your hands say out loud:

"Blessed be the energies of growth! I ask that the energies of this full moon bless this potion and that it bring joy, refreshment and vitality to all who use it!"

Hold the bottle of essential oils in your hand. Breathe deeply and imagine sunshine, warmth and happiness entering the bottle through your hands.

Now place the salt mixture in some pretty jars or bags. Place under the next new moon for blessing. Then add 5-7 drops of the potion to the salt jars just before using or gifting them.

Ritual for Lunar Connection

This spell can be done on any moon cycle but full moon is best. Mondays (moon days) are especially good.

Do the spell outdoors and it can be done at night, especially at moonrise. You might like to wear something white or silver.

You'll need:

- A white or silver bowl filled with water
- Wine or mead
- White candle

Stand up. Look right at the moon if that is available to you. Light the candle, saying as you do so:

> "Hail to you, Mani!
> I stand here before you as my ancestors' ancestors would have,
> Humbly honouring your power and beauty.
> Thank you for your light!"

Now imagine in your mind the moon and the way it waxes and wanes. It is never still but it is constant. See this cycle clearly.

Now offer the libation of wine or mead and say:

> "Shining One, I ask to be more deeply connected to your cycles for my benefit.
> I ask that my health improves, my use of time, my vitality increases, my mind to be sharp and kind and that I use the energies of the cycles well and benevolently.
> Please guide me in your wisdom."

Give thanks to Mani as all will be as you have asked.

Blow out the candle but leave the bowl with the water in it under Mani all night.

This water will be especially moon charged and you can use it in other spells, in baths and to drink for health and blessings.

Waning Gibbous 1

Themes:

KNOW THYSELF. SELF-REFLECTION. BE CURIOUS ABOUT WHO I AM. CHOOSE TO TURN INWARDS TO QUIETLY CONTEMPLATE WHO AND WHAT I AM AND WANT. NOT BEING AFRAID OF OUR DARKNESS. SLOWING DOWN.

Both scientists and spiritual practices believe that there is much benefit to be had in self-reflection. The process involves us thinking about what is happening, how we react and making sense of it. It exposes our strengths and weaknesses and gives us information to make changes if we choose to. It gives us a small respite in the busyness of life and allows our brain to make some sense of the chaos we experience each day.

Whilst self-refection is something we all would benefit from doing, why don't we do it? Firstly, self-reflection requires us to slow down somewhat and turn our awareness inward, something that does not come naturally to some, especially the highly extroverted. Not knowing exactly how to self-reflect can also be an issue. Starting small and maybe getting assistance with someone else as a guide can solve this. Perhaps a regular five-minute recap of the day as you commute home or before dinner, to sitting quietly to think about all that has happened and your reaction to it on this moon every moon cycle, to journaling how you feel each day. There are many ways and one will suit you.

The theme of waning gibbous moons, and this is the first, is the process of self-reflection and building resilience.

Self-reflection Spell

This spell can also be done at any time the moon is waning.

Ensure the room is warm or that you are safe and comfortable outdoors.

Ensure that you will be undisturbed.

Have your intention clearly in mind or written down.

Welcome the goddess and thank her for being with you here tonight in this beautiful place.

You'll need:

- Orange or white candle
- Matches
- Incense
- Pen and paper
- Basket of harvest fruits or grains to set the scene

Focus

Cast and open a circle if you wish or simply just light the candle.

Take several deep breaths. Close your eyes.

Think back on the past year. Take your time doing this.

Reflect back on the last 12 months. Visualise some of the key learning situations of the year so far. The good and what you consider the not so good.

Be detailed about this. See, touch, taste, smell, be in that time and place. Ensure that even with the more unpleasant situations you know there is a definite lesson there to learn and you have done this.

Building Power

Now, face the moon if you can.

Write down all those things that you can be grateful for that have occurred over the past year. List them one by one, or even draw symbols of them.

Get excited about the bounty and lessons you have received from everything you have 'planted' and worked hard for.

Look at the candle or close your eyes and go within.

See this and FEEL this gratitude and what richness it brings to your life. See how you grow from this harvest of your life. Feel your personal vitality. Feel it warm you, pulse through you.

Now light your incense.

Breathe in deeply. As you breathe in, you are inhaling even more power from the earth, the trees, the moon, and the sky.

The goddess is still with you accepting your gratitude and celebrating what is good for you.

Accept these gifts in your own body. Allow these energies to begin to mingle... yours and those of the goddess. Feel your own strength and that of the goddess course through you.

In a loud, firm voice say:

"I let go of anything that is a blind spot or not worthy of me."

Then chant:

"I reap what I sow
I watch as I grow
The harvest is deep
Forward I leap!"

Repeat the chant faster and faster at least three times, feeling your gratitude and energy grow.

Ask now to be told of what you need to do in the future to increase the bounty of your harvest. Write this down.

Continue chanting if your energy drops.

At the height of your energy hold it and SHOUT:

> "I reap what I sow!
> I watch as I grow!
> I reap what I sow!
> I watch as I grow!"

Know that the goddess/universe has heard your intention and gratitude.

Be grateful in the knowledge that all is as you have asked it to be, if it be Her will and for the greatest good of all. Know your mind and body are already responding.

Blow out your candle.

Close your circle.

Extinguish and bury any remaining incense in the garden or yard.

Ground yourself by eating or drinking something, exercising, or dancing!

Take a few steps towards continuing your project or to remain in gratitude in the real world. Do this within 48 hours of this spell.

Waning Gibbous 2

Themes:

FIND YOUR PLEASURE AGAIN. ARE WE ALL TOO SERIOUS RIGHT NOW? SEEK PLEASURES.

Seek light heartedness. Focus on what would make you happy. Schedule in activities that you find pleasurable.

In our search for a better life, something happened along the way. We forgot how to find real pleasure in what we do rather than just be diverted from the every day. We wait for holidays, rather than see the opportunities to let our mind and body rest in joy every day.

In the pagan philosophy a big part of pleasure is 'letting go'. This does not mean surrender as in 'give up' – it simply means to hand over all of our administration, our stress and our worries for a time, and immerse ourselves in something joyful. We see that without allowing ourselves to experience pleasure, whether it take the form of laughter, play, sensuality or the development of skills, that we remain less than whole and in a state of wanting.

Our ancient ancestors knew the importance of pleasure in the forming of a healthy mind, body and spirit. There were gods and goddesses dedicated to happiness and the pleasures of life. Take the Egyptian Goddess Hathor, for example. The temples of Hathor were joyful places, full of songs and beauty. There were even small temples placed in her honour outside other major deities' temples so that people could be in a happy and contented mental mood before entering to worship in other temples. The Egyptians clearly believed that having a positive or relaxed state of mind assisted in having a positive spiritual connection.

Developing practices that enable us to increase our playfulness and curiosity can not only make us happier but help us retain a good level of physical and mental energy. This means we can feel empowered even under difficult circumstances.

Finding your Pleasure

Many of us have forgotten what our true pleasures are. We work hard! We often have little time to really consider what makes us happy, deeply happy, right now. This is a simple but powerful ritual to explore with Dionysus. The best time for this ritual is night-time on this moon or a full moon.

You'll need:

- A white or green candle
- 2 glasses
- Wine or grape juice
- Paper and pen

Dress in something that you find beautiful and comfortable.
Light a candle and say:

"I humbly call upon Dionysus, Liberator!"

Now pour some wine in the first glass and offer it to Dionysus saying out loud:

"Thrice born son of Zeus, I offer this sacred wine to you!
Lakkhos, show me my pleasure!"

Now pour a smaller amount in your glass and say:

"Thrice born son of Zeus, I raise my glass to you!
Lakkhos, show me your blessing!"

Take a small sip.
Now shut your eyes. Think of a time when you experienced pleasure intensely. Take your time. Allow this feeling to flood through you.
Now say:

> *"I know pleasure. I want more of it. How best might I find it and experience it in a beneficial way, Dionysus? Please show me now!"*

Notice the answers or the feeling. Write these down. Or perhaps you may feel like moving or dancing – this too gives us hints to what will make us feel more pleasure.

Stay in the feeling of pleasure for as long as you like.

When you are ready, thank Dionysus and blow out the candle. Finish your glass if you like but leave his there. After a day or so, empty his wine into the garden.

Act upon the suggestions made.

Spell for Play and Pleasure

This spell features the cat-headed Egyptian Goddess Bast.

Ahead of time, think about one activity that you find makes you happy or playful. Hint: Often things we find a little 'silly' like dancing or singing out loud can be playful. Then think about where you feel unbalanced and stuck and where having some of Bast's help would be of assistance.

Outdoors is best for this spell if possible.

You'll need:

- ☾ A small candle
- ☾ Some incense
- ☾ If you have a cat, a small amount of already shed fur is a nice offering to this goddess

Light the candle and say out loud:

> *"Hail to you, Great Cat-headed Goddess Bast! I honour your loving playfulness, your watchful protection and your deep and abiding curiosity.*

Thank you for listening and being here."

Light the incense and leave the cat fur as a gift.

Take a deep breath and place your awareness into your feet for a moment. Imagine that they are extending the earth a little, like the roots of a tree. Continue to breathe and extend your energy down in a grounded way. Now think about being playful – doing the things that make you feel light and happy. If this is hard, think about a kitten or cat playing in the garden.

Feel the power of play. Feel how pleasant that feels. Feel the power of this.

Now pump this feeling up – its joy and lightness – permeating and lighting up every single cell. EVERY SINGLE CELL!

Keep breathing and taking in this energy. Now allow the aspects of your life that are keeping you low or stuck to simply leave your body as there is no room for them. Just be curious about this. Just watch and feel it all leave. You need not try to do this, just allow it – there is simply no room for anything that is a burden or heavy.

You should feel nothing now but lightness and excitement!

Open your eyes and leap up three times, as big a jump as you can make it, and say "YESSSSSS!"

Then say:

"Great Bast! I feel the balance that play and curiosity make to me. I will honour you by (say what you will do to play more often; this can be as simple as making a weekly play date with yourself!)"

Thank Bast.

Blow out the candle.

Action your play promise by scheduling the time in.

Waning Gibbous 3

Themes:

Seek balance. Seek moderation and reject extremes. Ground yourself and allow your strength to rise from there. Be aware of where the imbalances are in your life at present.

Working with the lunar cycle on a regular basis helps us actually experience the flow and balance of nature. The moon shows us the gradual and peaceful process of waxing and waning and the phases of perfect balance within. We also happily have the equinoxes, the balance of light and dark in the seasonal cycles. Our bodies, our minds and our human spirit seeks balance, yet perfect balance is almost impossible to achieve.

Think on this – if we stand on one leg and wish to balance ourselves, no matter how good at balancing on one leg we may be, it is a kind of dance, is it not? The large and small muscles in our legs adjust to keep us upright, always moving, never perfectly still. The rest of our bodies too are performing a myriad of adjustments, a little to the right here in one moment, a little to the centre here... The point is that balance is a process. It is something we can actively seek if we are wise, and additionally, we need to know when we are unbalanced so we can return to homeostasis.

Creating a Crystal Mandala for Balance with Vishnu

I love the mindfulness of creating mandalas. You can make them out of anything really – but making them with crystals and natural objects I think is the best. With this mandala, we will create one that expresses and resonates with the supremely balancing energy of Vishnu.

Decide on the size of your mandala and basic shape, but don't worry if you don't have it completely clear in your mind... that will happen as you begin to create.

You'll need:

- 20 or more crystals... I prefer blue and clear stones for Vishnu. Try a mix of raw and polished clear quartz, blue agate, azurite, lapis, and aventurine
- Special stones can include spiralite, volcanic glass or even aquamarine
- The lotus is the flower of Vishnu so if you can get your hands on one to include all the better
- I also would add objects that represent balance to you

Gather all crystals and objects carefully in a soft cloth and hold them, breathing deeply and visualising what it is that you would make. Consider also your intention for this grid and ask for the blessing of Vishnu.

Light a candle and burn some incense, sandalwood is particularly good. Allow the smoke to bless the stones.

Now choose the central stone, tell the stone what you would like it to do, in this case, radiate balance. Breathe upon the stone, enlivening it, place the stone with intent and then work outwards in any pattern and order which feels it is aligning with your intent.

When you are completed, place your own hand just above the whole mandala and say:

"Lord Vishnu, I feel your balance
To my left
To my right
Above me
Below me
Everywhere you are
I am."

Thank Vishnu and leave the mandala in situ as long as you wish.

Waning Gibbous 4

Themes:

BEAUTY IS LIKE MEDICINE: IT CAN HEAL EVEN THE MOST BROKEN SPIRIT. BEAUTY IS EVERYWHERE IN NATURE. THE OBSERVATION OF BEAUTY CAN CHANGE OUR VIBRATION AND STATE INTO SOMETHING HIGHER. BEAUTY COMES IN MANY FORMS.

One of the high needs I have in my life is that of beauty. I need to be exposed to what I find beautiful often to be at my best. You might find that a strange need, but it's far from uncommon, especially amongst creatives and artists.

Beauty to me isn't lots of make-up, or fancy skincare, or society's current beauty ideal. For me, beauty is nature and having things I find beautiful in my environment. These are not big things but often a flower, the twinkle of a star, the colour of my cat's eyes, the nail polish I just bought shimmering on my hands. All are expressions of beauty, they raise my mood. They give joy to my eyes, my heart and my mind. Everyone can experience beauty every day if they choose to look.

One of the important differences between the ancient pagan and the modern idea of beauty is that the old ways state there is a need for the core of the self to be developed and strengthened to enable and foster true beauty. This is an important two-way double punch as there is a strong mind-body connection when it comes to both beauty and vitality. Yes, whilst it is acceptable to use therapies that treat or beautify externally, it's equally important to stop bad habits that are detrimental to health and will interrupt the good you are doing.

Real beauty is hypnotic, yet in reality has less to do with youth than the spirit coming through the skin. The word 'charisma' comes from the Greek 'karis' and 'ma' meaning the spirit shining through. Each of us possesses a unique beauty, one that gives us confidence if we recognise it. This moon encourages us to bathe in beauty.

Loving My Body Ritual

Witches believe that loving our bodies is all about loving ourselves more and reducing fear. You may think this ritual is simple, but believe me, it changes every woman for the better and in particular, brings balance to the body. This can include benefits like weight loss, a lessening of stress-related illness and better skin.

You'll need:

- Some deliciously fragrant body moisturiser or massage oil

Do this every morning after your shower for the next 28 days and begin immediately!

Casting:

Have a shower or bath as usual and towel dry.

Then starting with your toes, apply the moisturiser or oil to your body and at the same time speak your word on why you love each part of your body. Do this quickly and do not hesitate!

For example, as you massage your toes say out loud:

"I love my toes because... and you must think of a reason you love your toes. For example: I love my toes because I can paint my toe nails different colours!"

Then go next to your feet: "I love my feet because... For example, they take me where I want to go." Then continue with your ankles, calves, knees etc., all the way to the hair on your head. Be sure to include your voice, your heart and your mind.

It's up to you what your reasons are but find something wonderful to say. No negatives allowed!

Now be aware there will be parts of your body you really can't think of much to express your love about. However, these are the bits we particularly have to love. So fake it till you make it on those parts. Stay with it and very quickly something positive will become natural for you.

Waning Gibbous 5

Themes:

MAKING MISTAKES BUILDS RESILIENCE. MISTAKES ARE LEARNING OPPORTUNITIES. STANDING STRONG, HEAD HIGH. I AM AN ADULT AND I ACT WITH SELF-RESPONSIBILITY.

Know as we stretch and expand towards our intentions, we will, most likely meet resistance or – wait for it – make mistakes or even fail. How will we view this 'failure'? Will we recover from our mistake?

This is where resilience, confidence and our inner will come into play.

Whilst all of us at some time have to go through periods of imbalance and difficulty, yes even of suffering, I think it is important that we learn to grow and rely on our resilience. This is true power from the inside out. Building and having resilience allows us the solidity yet the freedom to grow and to take that leap to the next level. It allows us to reach higher, with a stability that makes things less of a risk and allows us to create with a bit more pleasure.

Remember, mistakes are simply information gathering. That's it. The less drama and guilt and shame you can attach to them the better. The story of failure or mistakes should be one of learning – that is all. As we move around the lunar cycle and in life, we can see how things may have occurred before and that we now have experience in how to handle them.

Waning Gibbous 6

Themes:

Wisdom is more than knowledge, it is gathered and it takes time to develop. There may be something you aren't seeing – do more research. Gather good and wise people around you as allies. Good decision making.

It is often said that the body has its own innate wisdom. If healthy, it just knows what to do and it does what it needs to do to keep us alive and moving without us thinking too much about it. Most of the time, we don't think about trying to keep our heart beating, or how we keep breathing when asleep.

Similarly, we have this innate reasoning system, intuition, that allows us to get answers or receive information without conscious 'thinking'. It's that 'feeling' or 'hunch' of information or insight that comes. Some people believe that this is the wisdom we receive from the gods, the very spark of the divine voice that is left within us. This is a very old kind of wisdom that sits in a very old part of the brain.

Then there is the gathering of knowledge and experience and what we discern and learn from this. If the result has acuity, if it is successful in the real world and in good sense and good perception, well it's probably wise.

The getting of true wisdom usually takes time, and most often we are impatient for it. We might cut corners and not see the role we take in our own poor decision making. To me, though, as modern people, we have millennia of wisdom to assist us. Human history has some very wise people starring in it... and some not so wise... so we have plenty of examples to learn from. Gathering wiser people than we are around us is in fact one of the wisest things anyone can do!

Ritual for Wise Strategy

Athena is a wonderful deity to do spells with. She loves to assist those who wish to take action!

You'll need:

- ◯ 2 tablespoons of olive oil in a small dish
- ◯ A sprig of rosemary or a bay leaf
- ◯ Picture or statue of an owl (or if you are very lucky an owl feather)
- ◯ Bowl of salted water
- ◯ Piece of metal or metal jewellery to be used as a talisman
- ◯ Incense
- ◯ White candle

Place the owl picture near the candle. Light the candle and say:

"Bright-eyed Athena, you who are wise and beautiful, you who are strategic beyond measure, assist me tonight and grant me wisdom and good strategy."

Place the oil and rosemary/bay in front of the candle and say:

"I humbly offer you these gifts."

Light the incense.
Put your hands in the bowl of salted water and say:

"I wash away all that did not serve me this financial year and I purify my intent."

Now tell Athena exactly in which areas you need her wise counsel and help. Remove your hands and hold the talisman. Pass it through the incense and say:

> *"Athena, grant me the power to make good decisions and to take action to help myself and others. May I always have faith in myself and in you."*

Now ask Athena:

> *"What would you like me to do to take wise action towards?"*

The first thing that comes to mind, action.

Thank Athena.

Allow the candle to burn down and leave the offering there for 48 hours and then leave in nature. Wear or keep your talisman with you.

Last Quarter Moon

Themes:

EXPRESSING AND FEELING GRATITUDE. BE WHERE YOU ARE AND BE THANKFUL. GRATITUDE RAISES A LOWER VIBRATION TO A HIGHER ONE. FOCUS ON WHAT YOU HAVE WORKING FOR YOU. LIFE IS CONSPIRING FOR YOU.

As we enter the last quarter moon of the lunar cycle, the energies begin to turn towards surrender and release. To let go of what we no longer need, it behoves us to pay attention to what we have right now, positive and negative.

This paying attention and focus allows us to wisely discern and to be grateful for all of it. Yes, all of it. Because the nasty stuff, the stuff that is making you suffer right now, well it happened and we can take the wisdom from this, but now it's going (yes, the waxing crescent 4 and the dark moon is going to sort that for you). What we have left is the good stuff, and frankly, most of it is going to be good.

Taking some time out on this moon to just list a few things you feel grateful for will raise your vibration and banish any resistance you have to ditching old, outmoded patterns. Doing this also turns your powerful focus away from a story you may have started to believe of 'everything going wrong' or that 'life does terrible things TO you'. Gratitude is a balancer… in fact, it normally tips the scales to the positive.

Gratitude with Gaia

Go into a favourite place in nature, one that speaks to you of groundedness, earthiness and of Gaia. This must be outdoors – you cannot do this meditation indoors.

Light a green candle and say:

> *"Gaia, the oldest mother of all,*
> *Allow me to join with you now,*
> *Allow me to feel your green energy through my heart!"*

Begin to breathe slowly and deeply, slowly becoming aware of the relationship to the environment around you. If you are a woman, you may like to begin to take your breathing down through the belly into the womb. Imagine breathing in and out through this sacred place of creation. If you are a man connect and breathe through your sacral zone (extreme lower back).

Now begin to open all your senses to Gaia… extending yourself and reaching out to her like roots would search through the soil. Pull up some energy just like the roots would pull up water and nutrients.

Next, activate your vision: look around you, open your peripheral vision, also look at the detail… from the tiniest insect to the expanse of the sky. Soak in what you see and give thanks to Gaia.

Then go to your aural sense. Close your eyes and concentrate on the sounds around you. Listen closely to the layers of life. Be very still and listen to your heartbeat and the way it melts into her soundtrack. Again, give thanks to Gaia for her connection with you.

Now your sense of smell: breathe in with purpose! Smell the flowers, the greenness, the soil, the air.

Continue this through the other senses – taste and touch.

When you have connected completely this way, make a mental and physical note of the grounded feeling that you have... very connected, stable and secure... and grateful.

You can come back to this feeling any time.

When you are ready, thank Gaia and begin to release and come back to yourself. Know that you are changed and energised.

 # Waning Crescent 1

Themes:

YOU ARE LOVED AND PROTECTED. IDENTIFY YOUR FEARS, YOU CAN PROTECT YOURSELF BETTER. TRUST IN YOURSELF. YOU CAN HEAL YOURSELF.

As the lunar cycle comes to the last set of crescents, in this case the waning ones, we know that dark moon is close and so is the fresh start of the beautiful new moon.

Here is our chance to let go of our resistance, surrender and let go! To do that with confidence, we may feel that we need some support from the universe (or whatever we believe our higher power is). That support can take the form of feeling protected from whatever might happen and to help us get the courage to release what needs to go.

Witches and other pagan practitioners that use the lunar and seasonal energies often are asked to assist people with spells, techniques and even talisman of protection. These darker moons and the dark moon itself is a great time to create and cast for this purpose. An easy way is to plug into the earth, raise that benevolent and loving energy and turn to the four directions, asking each direction to shield and protect you in your endeavours. Then, finally, connecting with the moon herself, with you as conduit in the middle, full of power and confidence.

Trust in yourself to do what you need to do.

The Worry Jar

This is one of my favourite family spells that everyone can contribute to.

This spell can be started at any time but is most powerful on the waning part of the moon cycle.

Get a large jar with a tight lid. Feel free to decorate it on the outside if you wish but this isn't necessary.

Cut up lots of strips of paper and keep them in a bowl by the jar. Now, think about what your worries or anxieties are. Write a worry on each strip of paper and pop it in the jar. As you pop the worry in the jar say out loud:

"I call upon the power of winter. All my worries are captured and quiet. I have no need for them now. They now have no power whatsoever. They have no use and they die back. I know the universe will make this so!"

When you are done close the lid tightly then put the jar in the fridge.

As worries come up for you (or members of your family), the jar can be removed from the fridge, a worry written on a slip of paper and put into the jar. It should then be put back into the fridge.

When three moon cycles have passed, take the jar out of the fridge and carefully, so you don't lose any of the slips, pop them in a flame-proof bowl and set them alight! The fire of spring is now here to transform your worries into space for creative good!

Waning Crescent 2

Themes:

UNDERSTAND HOW RESISTANCE SHOWS UP FOR THE OVERT AND COVERT. IF YOU CONTINUE TO HAVE DOORS SLAMMED IN YOUR FACE, TURN AROUND; THERE IS NORMALLY AN OPEN DOOR. PROCRASTINATION IS JUST ANOTHER KIND OF FEAR. WE CONTROL OURSELVES AND NO ONE ELSE.

There are two kinds of resistance. The first type we encounter when we keep getting obstacles placed in our way or our way is blocked. For example, we try and get a particular job in a particular field and no matter what we do, it doesn't happen. This is a kind of external or overt resistance.

Covert resistance is somewhat sneakier. This kind of resistance is when you actually say you really want to do or complete something but you feel resistance not to. All forms of procrastination fit in here. Writer's block is a classic example. When you say you want to do something but you get distracted and you don't do it, or you just can't seem to engage your will enough, that is covert resistance.

When you want to get rid of a bad habit, an addiction, an old pattern, in fact anything that you are thinking of releasing for dark moon, and you feel resistance in doing so – you have a big dose of covert resistance.

We must battle this second kind of resistance like we would battle a huge, crafty and terrible enemy. We must raise our shields and sharpen our swords and have a strategy to remove the resistance. In fact, we must flow through it, after all, we ARE worth it. It's a battle we might have to fight more than once, but we will be resilient and vigilant and fight it. For if we win (and we will win), the rewards are great.

Shapeshifting Resistance Ritual with help from the Nature Spirits Called the Vila

You must do this outside under the moon.

You'll need:

- ❍ Flowers or small, sweet cakes – or both – as an offering to the Vila
- ❍ A white candle and matches
- ❍ Write down exactly what you wish to transform and what the resistance is
- ❍ Dress in something white or blue
- ❍ 2 pretty coloured ribbons of about 60 cm in length each

Casting:

Take all the items and go outside.

Take a long, deep breath and connect with the natural world around you. Look up at the sky and the sun, observe the trees, listen for the birds, feel the wind upon your skin.

Light the candle and say:

> *"Blessed are you the Vila! I bring gifts for you..."*
> (Push forward the plate of cakes or the flowers)
> *"Defenders of the forests, shapeshifters extraordinaire, I call upon you to assist me to change and transform my life."*
> *"I wish to transform my life in these ways: (Read out your list and tell the Vilas why these changes are important to you. Tell them also where your*

resistance is and ask them to transform these or take them away.)"
"I accept your guidance and help. I promise to participate in your name."

Now take the two ribbons and allow the wind to blow through them. (If there is no wind, just move them back and forth!) Say:

"As the wind and air lift these ribbons, I am reminded of your blessings, the freedom I have to act differently and of my change."

Now tie one ribbon to a high branch of a tree so the wind can catch and lift it. The other one should be tied to a doorway or fence outside.
Then say:

"I trust all will be as I have asked and I thank you again!"

Blow the candle out.
Take one real action towards your transformation, no matter how small, within 24 hours of performing this ritual.

Waning Crescent 3

Themes:

SURRENDER! SURRENDERING DOESN'T MEAN GIVING UP, IT'S LETTING GO OF WHAT YOU NO LONGER NEED. STOP BEING SO STUBBORN ABOUT HOLDING ON TO ASPECTS AND BEHAVIOURS THAT DON'T ALIGN WITH WHO YOU ARE NOW. STOP STRUGGLING.

It took me a long time to realise that surrendering was a positive thing. Now don't get me wrong. I don't mean the 'giving up' kind of surrender. I mean the 'Ok, it's time for me to hand this over' type of surrender.

For those of us who are highly independent and used to doing most things quite ably on our own, admitting we need assistance or that we might indeed have to let something go for our betterment can be challenging. For letting go and surrendering admits or exposes a vulnerability or two! To surrender, we may need to show our underbelly. We need to admit we may have got it wrong, made a mistake, grown a bad habit, surrounded ourselves with people that are not good for us or some other 'dumb' mistake.

But remember, this moon phase is dark and beautiful. It casts a protective shadow that allows us to be as wide open as we need to be to do our work. We reveal safely to only the divine and ourselves, and then the light returns.

Removing Negative Energy with Aradia

There is an art to letting burdensome energies go and to clearing negative energy if it is apparent. This spell is a beautiful, somewhat traditional spell that removes the negative energy and allows us the space to create something new or to simply heal.

This spell should be cast in your home near a front door.

You'll need:

- A red or black candle
- Small fabric bag filled with these dried herbs: rue, rosemary, sage, wormwood
- Besom (that's a broom!)
- Moon water (that is a bowl or jar of water put out under the full moon and placed in the fridge afterwards to keep fresh)
- Gift for Aradia e.g. a fresh flower, a pretty crystal

Light the candle and say:

"Daughter of Diana, I call upon you, Aradia! You who dance in the name of all that is divine, you who teach and lead, you who walk the path of magic for all. Please assist me now!"

Hold the bag of herbs to your heart and say:

"Rosemary and sage
Wormwood and rue,
By the power of Diana
Darkness remove!"

Take three pinches of herbs from the bag and sprinkle them on the floor throughout the room.

Now take the besom and take a deep breath and know that you will be sweeping away negativity now. Keep your focus and as you sweep keep saying:

"I sweep away what I no longer need,
I sweep clean my heart and home."

Sweep all the herbs outside your home and allow them to go into the garden. If you are in an apartment where the herbs will go into a corridor or foyer, sweep the herbs onto a newspaper and place in the garbage.

Now thank Aradia for her help and offer her the gift. You can place this on your altar or in a place of beauty outside.

Waning Crescent 4

Themes:

RELEASE. LET. IT. GO. REALLY. TOTALLY. ANYTHING THAT DOES NOT SERVE YOU, IT IS TIME TO RELEASE. YOU ARE READY TO MAKE ROOM FOR BIGGER, BRIGHTER, MORE ALIGNED THINGS.

Here we are, almost at dark moon, and surely you can feel it. The relief of dropping what has been burdensome to us. Make no mistake, stuff we no longer need – outdated emotions, beliefs and even physical stuff – is heavy. And yes, we might be tired carrying around all this quite ugly stuff that doesn't do anything great for us anymore.

Are you ready to put it down? Leave it? Not come back for it? Stand up straight for the first time in a long time?

Yes. I bet you are.

So do it. Begin the process. Allow yourself to dream of something lighter, stronger, better, happier.

Spell for Accepting Change

This spell is best cast on a waning cycle or dark moon and outside in nature.

Ahead of time, think carefully about what areas you are having a challenge, accepting a change. For example, a relationship that has ended and you are finding that hard to accept, a new school or job that you are worried about.

You'll need:

- ◐ An autumn-toned candle (red, orange, brown, gold)
- ◐ Wear something in the same colours
- ◐ Stick of incense or resin blend on charcoal
- ◐ Long orange or gold ribbon (say a metre long) – write your 'change' on it
- ◐ Tree or bush with branches low enough to tie the ribbon on

Light the candle and incense and say:

> *"Universe, I am truly grateful for the current harvest of my life! I am so delighted that I have (state great things in your life). Thank you! However, I am afraid of/finding certain changes challenging."*

Hold the ribbon:

> *"I fear/find challenging these changes and I am where I am. I would like things to be different, but until they are, I wish for me to live my life in joy and flexibility."*

Now tie the ribbon to the bush or tree... let it flow outwards catching the wind. When you are done, say:

> *"Universe! May the winds of change keep things flowing for me. Free me from fear and inflexibility. Let me know I can let things go easily and transform my life into something new."*

Thank the universe.
Allow your candles to burn down in safety.

Waning Crescent 5

Themes:

A DREAMY MOON OF PEACE. PEACE OF MIND IS ONE OF THE GREATEST GIFTS WE CAN GIVE OURSELVES. REFUSE DRAMA. DO NOT INVOLVE YOURSELF WITH CHAOTIC AND GOSSIP-SPEAKING PEOPLE. STOP FIGHTING, ALLOW YOURSELF TO REST FOR A WHILE.

When we let what we no longer need go, we make room for peace. We are an anxious bunch, us modern folk. We are constantly stimulated or not stimulated enough, we find it hard to sleep (insomnia is at record levels in the western world), and for some, we self-medicate with food, devices, drama and work. We seek peace but we don't know how to go about it particularly well.

Peace can begin with a series of decisions we make. For example, we can decide that we can't control everything. (Shock!) The ancient Greek Philosophy School of the Stoics has a great strategy here. They advise to split your page into two columns. One column is headed: 'I can control this'. The second column is headed: 'I have no control over this'. Now think about the most pressing and worrying issues you have right now or the situations that are giving you the most sleepless nights and break them down into pieces and place them in the correct columns. Be honest and discerning.

What you will find is most of your situations or issues are in the second column. The Stoics advise that the things listed in the second column deserve no more of your attention because they are actually out of your control. (Wow!) However, the things in the 'I have control' column, are important and you must action these to the best of your ability. These are the things that you will influence and where you will glean the most change. Whilst this seems a simple system, I promise you it will give you far less to worry about and instantly more peace.

On this moon we can attempt to be more focused and mindful about what we are doing in real time. We can place ourselves deliberately for sessions in quiet, beautiful and peaceful environments like sitting under the moon regularly. We can learn what, for us, brings our body rest and peace. We can choose to not do our head in with miles of worry. Worry is, after all, chewing gum for the mind – not really nutritious in any way, but something to do.

Meditation for Peace Featuring the Polynesian God of Peace Lono

There is an art to letting burdensome energies go and simply enjoying cultivating peace. We don't do this very often and Lono is the perfect deity to assist us to truly relax and appreciate the healing power of doing very little.

You will need to pick a night when there are stars or planets in the sky and pick a spot where you can lie down safely and watch them.

Put on something white in Lono's honour.

You'll need:

- O Some fruit for an offering
- O Salted water (a bowl of normal tap water with a handful of salt is fine)
- O A bowl of fresh water

Prepare an offering of tropical fruits.

Start by washing your hands in the salted water. Sprinkle some on your hair.

Then, take the bowl of fresh water and the offering outside to the spot you have chosen.

Connect with the earth and the night sky by lying down upon the earth and looking at the stars and the expanse of the sky.

If you like, you could sing or say this oli (chant), which is taken from the creation mythos of the mighty Kumulipo:

> "*Lewa Makalii, lewa Na-huihui (swings the Pleiades, swings the star cluster),*"

Then say:

> "*I am grateful and full of reverence for the gifts of the land and the sky. Lono, white-wearing and peace loving, I humbly ask to be connected with you and to honour you.*"

Now relax and allow your mind to focus on nothing but the swirls of the universe above you. Don't move your head. Just allow the sky and the stars and the moon (and anything else!) to simply float through your plane of vision. Breathe deeply. Allow your mind to make patterns in the sky if it wants, but no thoughts other than those of the sky.

If you catch your mind focusing on something else, simply direct it back to the night sky in a compassionate way.

Allow yourself to drift there for at least half an hour. Then when you are ready, sit up gently and thank Lono. Take the bowl of salt water and splash your face and then pour the fresh water into the earth with another expression of gratitude. You can pour the salt water down the drain when you come back inside.

HOW TO GARDEN
WITH THE MOON

There is so much lore around the moon and planting that you could simply create a big fat book just on this topic alone and there are probably Farmer's Almanacs that list planting suggestions for your area if you wanted to go down a more detailed pathway. For the purposes of this work, I'm going to give you a good grounding (excuse the pun) on how you can garden more successfully and magically by using the moon cycle.

Being a witch a thousand years ago meant that you would have a fine knowledge of herbal medicine. There was a great respect and honouring of these particular plants, and so wisdom on how best to plant and propagate them was vital to such a practitioner.

Herbs and other magical plants were so precious that only a boleen, a special crescent moon-shaped knife made from silver metal only used for harvesting the herbs, was used. I still use a boleen today for most herbs or plants I intend to use for magical purposes.

Today there are laws in most countries ensuring only trained herbalists, naturopaths and medical practitioners can prescribe botanical remedies for internal use. I am personally not a medical practitioner, and as such, legally cannot advise you to take any herbs, woods or flower derivatives internally or topically for health reasons. However, I want to introduce herbs and other plants to you in regard to the way they can work for you within magical rituals and spells for proven results.

Again, as in all moon-based working, observation is key – this time of your land (the area you will be gardening in) as well as the lunar cycle itself.

A really useful idea I learnt from my friend and permaculture expert, Miranda Mueller, is to keep a gardening journal over time, that you record sunlight, shadows, where it's particularly dry or wet, what insects, reptiles or birds seem to be about and when. All this information builds to give us a story of our place. Layer this with planting by the moon and we normally get a rich, lush and useful garden.

I would also suggest that you take some time to try and consult the indigenous people of your area for an even deeper map of what your country does and when. I am from Australia and our First Nations people have a powerful connection to country. Our aboriginal people have a 60,000-year-old complex relationship with their lands and so their close observation of the ecosystem over time is pretty unmatched.

How to use Waxing and Waning Cycles

As we learnt earlier in this book, we know that the moon controls the tides and influences water. The full moon pinnacle pulls the water the furthest upwards within the earth. The dark moon, the pinnacle of the waning cycle, has the water settle at its lower level, often within the reach of the roots of a plant or tree.

The Waxing Cycle and Full Moon

As the water rises and swells within the soil, this is a perfect time to plant seeds. It is also a good time to harvest some 'above the ground' plants at the peak of their goodness. For example, harvesting lettuce, kale, basil, fruits on trees during the end of the waxing cycle or during full moon, is optimum.

The Waning Cycle and Dark Moon

As the moon begins to wane, the water level sinks and there is less moisture in the soil. This is the time for planting and harvesting your 'below-ground' plants such as potatoes, carrots, onions, parsnips and beetroot. Prune and trim. Traditionally, dark moon is the optimum time for planting garlic and onions.

New Moon

Growth has slowed but will soon speed up again. A great time to plants seeds for above ground plants. Prune, trim and fertilise. Apply any necessary natural pest control.

Layering with the Zodiac Signs

If you like, you can further layer your moon magic working with 'fertile' or 'barren' astrological signs, but the most important lunar influence is the physical phases.

__'Fertile' zodiac signs__ are those that come under the elements of water and earth.

These are:

◖ Water: Cancer, Pisces, Scorpio
◖ Earth: Capricorn, Taurus, Virgo

Water and earth signs are considered the 'growth' times for plants. Water corresponds to the growth of leaves and green stems, earth corresponds with roots and bulbs.

__'Barren' zodiac signs__ are those that come under the elements of air and fire.

These are:

◖ Air: Libra, Gemini, Aquarius
◖ Fire: Aries, Leo, Scorpio

Air traditionally corresponds to flowers or blossoms. Fire corresponds to the process of seed development and fruiting.

As a rule of thumb, all your maintenance chores should be done during the times when the moon is in the fire and air signs. I particularly like to weed during fire sign influences as the plants seem to respond to this 'full stop'.

I love to turn my compost bins with intention on these moons.

I have also personally found that planting and harvesting from trees on air sign times is extra effective.

In regards to producing magic around the plants on these signs, here is how it works for me...

Let's say I decided to do some magic around clearing my home. I choose a couple of herbs or roots that would be good for that, which I have growing in my garden. Let's say I decide to use some garlic for protection, some sage for clearing and some rosemary for clarity.

I would decide the best time to cast the spell is the waning cycle or dark moon because this is the time where we ideally remove energy. I would, as garlic is a below the ground plant, harvest this on a dark moon or at least the late waning lunar cycle. The sage I would have harvested on a waxing cycle or new moon and the rosemary the same, ahead of time. This will mean all the plants will be at their lunar peak for that particular species.

If I could, I would try also to harvest the garlic on an earth sign, thus having the root at its best. I would harvest the sage on a fire or air sign because I'll be burning it and it is for the purposes of clearing. With the rosemary, I might have a preference for a water or air sign simply because of the properties of green in the plant and for the clearing of the intellect that rosemary does so well.

What would this magic look like?

Well, I would make a small offering plate of olive oil and some garlic and leave it overnight to steep. Next day, I would offer some on my altar to the Goddess Hekate, who is protective of the gateways and doorways of all kinds. I would also place a drop of the oil on the main doorways or gateways of my home. Using the incantation "Only the good and loving should enter here", I would then take the rosemary, strip the leaves from the stem and place the leaves in a bowl with two handfuls of coarse sea salt.

I would then toss the salt on the floors of the rooms of my home saying:

"As I throw, may the salt of the sea cleanse my home. May the leaves of rosemary make everything clear no matter where we roam."

Then sweep or vacuum up the salt and rosemary. The final step is to burn the dried leaf of sage and allow the fragrant smoke to drift through the house as a final purification.

Remember, all this layering of magic, as simple or as complex as you choose, along with your will, makes your intent real.

Boosting the Garden

You might want to add some tiny natural quartz crystal points to your gardening areas by burying them, especially those areas that don't look so fertile. I call this 'seeding' with crystals. I pop them in with my finger at about an index finger depth. They work even better if the crystals have been left under a full lunar cycle, the way I recommend in the next section on talismans.

Another booster is to save some of the aqua luna that I create each full moon for my garden, especially the plants that maybe aren't doing so well and need extra lunar energy. I might also give plants that I know I will soon be harvesting, especially for magical purposes, aqua luna.

I might also grid my property with 'wards' to protect it. A ward is a kind of protective incantation that creates a barrier around a property or home repelling negative energy and people with evil intent. The added bonus is that it creates a beautiful, calming and nourishing balance for the garden itself.

Here is a simple way to place a 'ward' around your home. This should ideally be done on a new or full moon. You can cast during the day.

Ahead of time work out the four corners to your property or go by the compass and find out the border spot to north, south, east and west. Know these spots.

You'll need:

- 4 quartz crystals or 4 black obsidian or 4 Herkimer diamonds that have been charged under a full and dark moon

Make sure you will not be disturbed.

Firstly, cast a circle and draw up energy into your body. Feel strong and full. Have the crystals in the circle with you. When you feel ready step out of your circle holding the four crystals.

Now walk to the north. Stand in the spot at the north, place the crystal in the ground and begin to walk along the boundary but to your spot in the east. As you walk say:

> *"I call upon the guardian of the north. And all benevolent genus loci of this place. I ask that you bring your focus and power to my words and will. I ask that I now make a protective barrier around this place, that my words be my ward, unbroken, unbounded and that no evil or harm shall cross this threshold."*

Now repeat this from east to west, from west to south, from south back to north. When you are back to north clap three times and say:

> *"So shall it be!"*

Then go back to your circle. Give thanks. Close your circle.

Plants and their Superpowers

There are so many amazing plants you can use in lunar magic and magic generally, but to make things a little easier, I have listed them in a handy format.

NAME		WISDOM OF THE PLANT
Acacia	H	Money, love, protection, psychic powers
Agrimony	H	Protection, peaceful sleep
Angelica	H	Banishes hostility from others, protection, healing, warming
Ash	W	Expansion of horizons, healing, strength, prosperity
Azalea	F	Hidden emotions, secrets
Basil	H	Love, exorcism, wealth, conquers fears of stepping up
Bay Leaf	H	Protection, psychic powers, healing, purification, strength and endurance
Birch	W	Cleansing, health, wisdom, new beginnings, lunar workings, protection of the young
Bladderwrack (Seaweed)	H	Protection against accidents or illness, especially at sea, sea rituals, wind rituals, action, money, psychic powers
Borage	H	Aids the expression of sorrow, grief. Strength
Cactus	F	Protection, purity
Calamus	W	Healing, protection, helps bind long distance lovers

(H) HERB (W) WOOD (F) FLOWER (S) STEM (B) BULB (O) OIL (L) LEAF (B) BARK (R) ROOT (V) VARIOUS

NAME		WISDOM OF THE PLANT
Caraway	S	Protection, passion, health, wisdom, mental powers
Catnip	H	Love, beauty, happiness in the home, fertility, appeal, cat magic
Chicory	H	Invisibility in hostile situations, removing obstacles, receiving favours, melts frigidity both mentally and physically
Chilli	F	Heats up waning relationships, brings problems to a head
Cinnamon	B O	Spirituality, success, healing powers, psychic powers, money, passion and love
Clover	L	Luck in love, happiness
Devils Shoestring	G	Wealth and protection
Dragons Blood	H	Love, magic, protection, dispels negativity, increases male potency
Eucalyptus	W O	Clarity, strength
Fenugreek	S	Attraction, seduction
Fig	F R W	Wisdom, creativity and creation, fertility, harmony and balance
Frankincense	R O	Worth, psychic powers, prosperity
Garlic	H	Aphrodisiac, protection and healing, banishing negativity, passion, warming and toning
Guinea Pepper	H	Dispels negativity
Hempseed	S	Marriage divination

NAME		WISDOM OF THE PLANT
Honeysuckle	F	Money, psychic powers, protection
Jasmine	F	Fertility, lust, seduction
Juniper	H W	Protection against negative forces, love, banishing negativity, health, increases male potency, purification
Ladies Mantle	H	Conception, restoration of natural menstrual cycle, protection
Lavender	H	Love, protection (especially of children), quiet sleep, long life, purification, happiness, peace
Lemon Balm	H	Calming, purification
Licorice	R	Good luck, cleansing, attraction
Lotus/Water Lily	F R	Protection, reveals secrets, sensuality, resilience
Lucky Hand Root	R	Employment, luck, protection, money, safe travel
Mandrake	R	Aphrodisiac, protection, love, money, fertility, health
Marigold	F	Protection, prophetic dreams, legal matters, increases psychic powers
Mint	H	Money, love, increasing sexual desire, healing, banishing
Mugwort	H	Fertility, female sexual organ tonic, healing
Oak	W	King of the waxing year and sacred tree of the Druids, supreme tree of knowledge, power and independence, confidence, prosperity, potency
Olive	W O	Peace and reconciliation, forgiveness, healing, fertility

(H) HERB (W) WOOD (F) FLOWER (S) STEM (B) BULB (O) OIL (L) LEAF (B) BARK (R) ROOT (V) VARIOUS

NAME		WISDOM OF THE PLANT
Orange	F O W	Love, abundance
Passionflower	F	Sacrifice, peace, quiet sleep, friendship
Pennyroyal	H	Female stimulant
Pine	W O W	Healing, fertility, purification
Poppy	F	Fertility, rest, money, luck, invisibility
Raspberry Leaf	FL	Fertility, uterine tonic, flexibility
Rose	F O	Aphrodisiac, beauty, connection, long-lasting love
Rosemary	H	Love, passion, increases mental powers, banishes negativity and depression, beauty
Rowan	W	A tree of the White Goddess of the Celts, domestic protection
Rue	H	Protective, keeps away curses and negative energy
Sage	H	Long life, wisdom, protection, purifies, fertility
Saffron	F S	Lust, fertility, higher love, money
Sandalwood	W	Protection, healing, banishes negativity, masculine strength
Sarsaparilla	H	Love, attraction
Snake root	H	Luck, money
Snapdragon	F	Keeping secrets, finding what is lost
Southern Wood	W	Masculine energy, lust, love
Squaw Vine	H	Feminine, balance, hormonal healer, solidness
St. John's Wort	H	Health, power, protection, strength, love and fertility, love, divination, happiness

NAME		WISDOM OF THE PLANT
Sunflower	F S	Developing potential, fertility, confidence, self-esteem
Tansy	H	Spring equinox herb, health, long life, conception/pregnancy
Tiger Lily	F	Purity of spirit, wildness
Valerian	H	Love, love divination, quiet sleep, purification, protection against outer hostility, inner fears and despair
Vervain	L	Lust, seduction
Violet	F	Modesty, secrecy, uncovering hidden talents
Walnut	W N	Intelligence
Willow	W	Traditional goddess tree, a moon tree, intuition, moon magic, healing, making wishes come true, increasing psychic energies, empathy
Witch Hazel	H	Mends broken hearts and relationships, finds buried treasure and underground streams, protection
Witchbane	W H	Protective, transformational, attracts good energy where there was a void of negativity
Witches Grass	H	Attraction, intensity, happiness, unhexing
Wormwood	L	Plant of Goddess Artermis, protective, purging, clearing, dream inducing
Yarrow	H	Courage, love, psychic powers, divination, assures long-term love, banishes negativity
Yucca	H	Transformation, change, protection, purification

(H) HERB (W) WOOD (F) FLOWER (S) STEM (B) BULB (O) OIL (L) LEAF (B) BARK (R) ROOT (V) VARIOUS

How are Plants Best Used in Lunar Magic?

Well, that depends on the plant and what you are doing.

In magic we do everything from burning, to making potions and infusions, to popping them in baths, to weaving them, to placing them in poppet or juju bags. We use the fragrant ones to make incense and oils, we literally sweep negative energy with some made into besoms (brooms) and we crown ourselves with flowers and leaves.

Some plants I use freshly picked (say for magical potion baths) but most are conserved by drying them. This preserves the energy and vital chemical compounds. To dry leaves and stems I normally tie a string to the bottom and hang upside down in a breezy place that is warm but out of direct sunlight. The airiness is important so that you don't attract mildew or your plants do not rot. Garlic you may have seen plaited together with their green long leaves and dried in windowsills and flea bane I use the same way.

The herbs should be well dried before you use them, especially if you are using them to stuff pillows or in incenses.

And so thinking about what plant energies you might want or need for yourself and your loved ones is important if you wish to do specific magic. There is also a case for simply planting a variety of plants that flower at night or have associations with deities of the moon or the night itself, to further enjoy and magnify the lunar experience if that is your goal.

In my own garden, I have night blooming jasmine, Japanese wisteria, Evening primrose, Datura (white morning glory), night blooming honeysuckle, Angel's trumpet, moonflower, gardenia, Artemisias and a cactus called Queen of the Night. Most of these plants have white or light-coloured flowers, which are thought to attract night-time pollinators like moths and bats.

I have often sat out on my open verandah to utiseta and watch the moon, surrounded by the heady fragrance of these plants and the creatures of the night they attract – all adding to the deep awe of the moment. All this contributes to the strength of my magic should I wish to partake.

Certain deities (gods and goddesses) are also associated with particular plants and you can use them to make offerings to these energies or in potions or talismans in their honour.

MOON DEITIES	PLANTS
Aphrodite	Rose, bladderwrack
Aradia	Forget me not, roses, magnolias, rue
Artemis	Artemisias: like wormwood, vervain, willow and oak
Athena	Olive
Brigid	Spring blossoms, rose, hay, yarrow, strawberry
Diana	Apples, vervain, mugwort, oak
Hekate	Garlic, mandrake, wolf's bane
Hina	Seaweed, white frangipani
Isis	Frankincense, myrrh, wheat
Lilith	Night flowering jasmine
Morgan Le Fae	Blackhorn, rosemary, wormwood, yarrow
Nuit	Night flowering plants, chickweed
Pan	Rosemary, mullein, figs
Thoth	Blue water lily
Tu'er Ye	Green vegetables, white cherry blossom

There are also certain key trees that we love to use in lunar workings. One is the willow. We see the willow as a feminine tree, lunar based in its growth cycle and one that can give us a model of growth and how we can be successful in life.

Think of a willow tree. Willows often grow on the sandy banks of highly shiftable and changeable rivers. Yet, they grow to huge sizes, successfully growing and holding fast in unpredictable habitat. How do they do this?

When you see a young willow on the banks, for a long while, it just looks like a feeble stick. It may have a few branches and leaves, but at first the trunk will be fine and flexible, rather than robust looking. What we don't see immediately is the root base.

The willow is spending a lot of time establishing a veritable root city under the surface. These roots are long and strong and numerous, finding their way into many nooks and crannies, holding onto rocks, other established tree roots and anything that can help with their stability. These roots go off in all directions, thus securing their position just in case the earth begins to shift. Then and only then, once these root networks are established well enough, does the willow puts its energy into further growth.

The trunk begins to thicken, widen and harden, and travel upwards to the sky. The branches however, as they grow, have little of the trunk's supportive thickness; they have instead the instruction that they must grow flexible. Flexible means they can turn with the sun and survive punishing winds that might threaten to topple the rest of the tree. All of this growth is done with purpose and a divine strategy.

Ramping Up the Power

Magic is meant to be layered with meaning and energy. It's like the alchemy in cooking – we add specific ingredients to make the magic of the dish as a whole. By layering our lunar energy even further with the big powers of deities and the divine animals we boost the power and reach of our magic far further than we could by ourselves.

DEITIES AND ANIMALS OF THE MOON

One of the aspects of lunar lore that I fell in love with pretty quickly as a young person was that of the gods and goddesses. I loved myths (the stories with a truth) even as a child. Yet as I grew I began to understand that these stories and art weren't just little fairy tales like the 'man on the moon', but they were so much deeper and more instructive than that. These deities could help me transform myself and flow forward, just like the moon phases did. These amazing queens, goddesses, gods and kings led by example, and boy, don't we all need good strong examples.

Witches believe that we each have a spark of the goddess and god within us. In natural reciprocity, the goddess and god have a spark of us within them. Knowing intimately that by having a spark of divinity within you, you are indeed goddess or god, tends to change reality for us. It is difficult to experience self-hate if you know that you have the divine within you. Self-esteem comes flowing back, flooding us with positive change if we truly come to this realisation.

The goddesses too can teach us self-trust, something else we might lack.

I love to ride horses, but as I learned to ride as an adult, I don't possess that complete lack of fear that the little girls have at the stables I visit. There are literally tens of them, aged between five and fifteen, confidently leading, galloping, jumping, maneuvering animals that are literally half a tonne in weight.

I watched as one eight-year-old girl spoke to her new friend as she faced a new jumping height on her mare, Red. She introduced herself as "Rhiannon, like the horse goddess" (someone with a pagan parent!). She examined the height intently as she led her horse to it. Both circled it like prey, and with a simple ease, they trotted back up to the starting point where her friend was waiting.

"Yep, we can do this," she said to her friend.

"Ooh it's a bit higher than the last one. You better be careful," her friend replied.

The girl smiled at her friend with shining eyes and said, "Yes, it is higher but I can lead Red to that, and I don't need to think about being careful. Red does that."

Off she went. Sailed over the jump like she had been doing it all her life. A huge smile and cuddle for her horse followed. And as I watched I knew that I had witnessed the unerring power of self-trust, rather than lack of fear.

The particular myth of the welsh goddess Rhiannon models what happens when we doubt ourselves and the queen we can become when we don't. This little girl no doubt embodied Rhiannon's example of self-trust in herself.

Almost every culture has a lunar goddess or god. From Polynesia's Hina to ancient Greece and Rome's Artemis and Diana, through to the dark goddesses of the night of Nuit and Isis, and Hekate, Ix Chel and Morgan Le Fae.

I am very privileged to have as my patroness a moon goddess. I also work with a dark moon goddess.

My patroness is the Greek Goddess Artemis. I loved her before I knew who she was. My mother had a perfume bottle that had a carved cameo of her – this beautiful athletic figure with a bow and arrow and big dogs under a crescent moon. Apparently, I kept taking this bottle and putting it under my pillow. My mum would retrieve it almost every day and I would take it back. Eventually she allowed me to have it and it sat pride of place on my dresser. One day my local librarian suggested a book on the Greek myths, and I cracked it open on the very same image of the same goddess. I learnt she was Artemis, Goddess of animals and the moon; she was sort of boyish and preferred to have her own realm of the forest. All this I instantly understood, after all, I was already in love with the natural world, the moon and the animals.

But it wasn't until I got older that I realised she could be a role model for me in other ways. Artemis was unashamedly independent, and this was in a world that wasn't used to seeing women in that way. My favourite myth about her involves her father Zeus, the king of the Olympians.

Zeus, although a god, had some favourites in the mortal world. His daughter, Artemis the Huntress, saved one of the mortals from certain death in one of her forests one night, and Zeus called forth his strong and capable daughter to reward her.

"Daughter, I wish to thank and reward you," said Zeus. "I wish to give you what women seem to want most – a good husband. Allow me to choose one that honours you and your status."

Speaking with her father about her future for the first time, she was quite horrified by the idea that she would have to marry at all, since she loves her wild life in the green places. And so, she begged Zeus to allow her to never marry but to remain a maiden, free of the confines of a home and to live wildly in the forests with just animals for company. She also asked that she be allowed to always wear a short tunic so she could be unhampered in her movement.

Zeus was profoundly moved by his daughter's authentic and stark admissions and granted her this unusual wish.

Now, as a goddess of animals and of the primal places like the forest, she receives the finest hounds from the god Pan, and these dogs are chosen for their unmatched abilities to bring down lions, catch the swiftest hares and mark the lair of the stag. She is so delighted with this gift that she is happy to allow Pan to share some of the realm and play his sweet music.

As you can see Artemis is unusual. She is independent, she knows what she wants, she is focused (those arrows) and she is a midwife to many but has no children of her own. She is intimately close to nature and all the cycles of the earth and moon. She punished those who broke the rules of nature or were cruel or hunted without reason. She was one of the first environmentalists in a way as lands that were sacred to her were kept as wild and untouched as possible.

To me, a young woman who didn't quite fit in, who had to work in male-dominated environments, who loved nature and animals, and who craved freedom and a different way forward than many – she was my go-to role model. Yes, being feminine and focused was possible. Being compassionate and looking after others didn't mean I had to have children of my own. Being an advocate for nature was important, just as important as being an advocate for people.

And so I learnt all I could about Artemistic temples and her ancient worship and cult. I began to include her in all my moon workings. Needless to say, pretty much everything improved, especially my personal power and confidence. I decided I would study with an Artemistic priestess in Greece through the temple system and learn all I could. I've now been dedicated to her longer than I haven't.

The dark goddess I work with is Hekate. Like most dark goddesses she is misunderstood. She was also one of the first goddesses I ever worked with and I remember very clearly going down to the crossroads near my house with a gift of garlic for her and with some of my dog's fur that had dropped off. I had to make a big life decision at the time and I didn't know what to do. I heard that she was the one to help you get off the place of paralysis when it came to decisions. She would show me which way to walk off that crossroads.

It was midnight, I was a bit scared and I was waiting for signs that Hekate would come. It is said that when you call her name thrice correctly and respectfully the wind will rise and dogs will bark. So here I was, a complete beginner under a dark moon in the middle of the night, wanting to pay my respects to an ancient Greek goddess who was admittedly a little scary.

I need not have worried. For Hekate is an illuminator of the dark. She shines her torch (one of her names is torch bearer and she lit torches for her friend Persephone to guide her home from the underworld) and she opens the doors to that which cannot be immediately seen (a symbol of hers is the key). So I learned the correct way to call her. I did. The wind rose, dogs indeed barked, and all the lights came on at the crossroads! I did my ritual. I got my guidance and I buried the garlic.

The next day, I made one of the best decisions of my life.

And therefore this triple-faced goddess is one I have an altar of devotion to in my home.

Do I recommend going down the lunar rabbit hole and learning about goddesses and gods and asking for them to lend you some energy? Yes, indeed. This, though, is a journey only you can go on. Yes, I can give you a list of deities but really the search is part of the magical journey.

Here are some deities I recommend working with that have links to the moon:

- Artemis (Greek)
- Aradia (Roman)
- Arianrhod (Welsh)
- Brigid (Celtic)
- Cerridwen (Welsh)

O   Diana (Roman)

O   Freyja (Norse)

O   Hina (Polynesian)

O   Mani (Norse)

O   Morgan Le Fae (Celtic)

O   Skadi (Norse)

O   Thoth (Egyptian)

O   Triple goddess (archetype, European Wiccan)

O   Yemaya (Yorbian)

Here are a couple of tried and tested rituals should you wish to engage with Artemis, Hekate or Yemaya. I have plenty more information on my website themodernwitch.com on goddesses and gods should you seek it.

Running with Artemis

Over many years of working with Artemis, I have found I connect with her very quickly if I am moving. She is quite the action deity so this makes total sense. If you can't run – just go as fast as you can go – the idea is to move through nature and not be stagnant.

The best moon phase for this is anytime on the waxing phase and daytime is fine. All you need is you and a small stone in the shape of an arrowhead. Look around for one or make it!

Decide on a walking or running route. Artemis loves the forest and the green, so you might choose a park, a bush walkway or even a well foliaged street. Also think about what you want Artemis' help with. Ideal things to ask for are assistance with focus, being independent or running your own race in life. If you have a dog (your very own hound!) you may wish to take them along too – Artemis loves her dogs!

Hold the arrowhead stone in your hand. Begin to walk and say:

> *"Artemis of the Moon, allow me to walk with you in your green home."*

Breathe deeply and focus on the feeling of your body travelling through nature.

Feel your muscles work and your body move. Also be very aware of your surroundings. The birds, the trees, the sounds, the temperature, the smells.

Begin to accelerate your walk to a jog, or if you are just keeping it at a walk, perhaps swing your arms a little more. Say:

> *"Artemis, I invoke thee! I too move through the green. I ask for your assistance with greater focus and also with... (insert your intention). You who are a protector and a huntress who never misses the mark, show me the way forward!"*

Keep moving, allow yourself to now go as fast as you can. Run if you can! At the peak of your energy say:

> *"Artemis, I join you! I connect and all will be so!"*

Now imagine placing some of that strength and power you have into the stone in your hand.

Say:

> *"I give you thanks!"* and bury the stone into the earth.

Invocation to Hekate

Be respectful!

This ritual can be done at any crossroads (where three pathways or roads meet).

As I approach the crossroads, I often like to call her name three times out loud. You will often hear a dog bark or the wind rise or whistle as you do this. This shows she is present.

You'll need:

- ○ 3 red candles
- ○ Some ground good quality incense like frankincense
- ○ Some dog fur (just pat your dog and collect the shed hairs)

Cast this at a crossroads. A simple crossroads is probably at the edge of your property where your path and gate meet the public path or at the end of your own street.

Light the first candle

Say:

> *"Great Goddess Hekate, bright headed, twin flamed!*
> *You who rule over the crossroads, our past present and future,*
> *The dark, the crescent and the full,*
> *Help me now,*
> *Illuminate my path,*
> *Show me the way!"*

Place the dog hairs at the crossroads and light the second candle.

> *"Great Goddess Hekate Apotropaia*
> *Of dark and night, many named!*
> *You who visit the underworld*
> *Show me the way through,*
> *Come what may!"*

Now ask Hekate to assist you with clarity and the illumination of issues in your life. Know the goddess is listening.

Light the third candle, and say:

> *"I pay you tribute almighty wise goddess, I ask that this small flame joins yours, spreading light to the darkest corners of my shadow. Bring me peace and wisdom and a resolution to my problems if it be for the good of all and your will."*

Now light the incense and let it burn down, relaxing in the energy at the crossroads.

Express your gratitude, blow out the candle and then leave only the dog hairs there.

Hekate: The Illumination Ritual

Light a candle and place a gift for Hekate including a shell and some garlic.

Ahead of time write down where you need support and/or guidance to go forward.

Roll this up in a ball and tie it with some red string.

Bury this in the ground. Add some honey to the top.

Ask Hekate for one action you can take. This may come in a dream or as an urge to take some kind of action.

Hekate: The traditional Deipnon (Hellenic)

The Deipnon consists of three main parts:

1. A meal that was set out at a crossroads, usually in a shrine outside the entryway to the home
2. An expiation sacrifice (a kind of personal penance or amends)
3. Purification of the household

Yemaya's Boats

This is a ritual based on the traditional activity of sending boats filled with wishes to Yemaya. This spell must be done by the sea or river on a new or full moon.

You'll need:

- Paper or leaves to make a boat
- A small tealight candle
- A gift to Yemaya: a pearl or a seashell (something silver)

Ahead of time think about your wish and have it in your mind in a clear concise fashion.

Make your little boat ahead of time. Write your wishes on the boat or draw symbols upon it representing those desires.

Place the candle inside but be careful you don't burn the boat when it's time to light it.

Carry it down to the water. Have your gift to Yemaya with you as well.

Say out loud:

"Yemaya, Yemaya, Yemaya!
Silvery Goddess of the Sea,

Moon blessed, she who responds,
Goddess of women and wishes, please hear my voice!
Yemaya, I ask you to grant my wish(es) and help me flow like the incoming
tide towards my highest good! I humbly offer a gift to you!"

Then throw the gift (shell etc) into the water.

Place your feet in the water. Now tell Yemaya of your wish. Don't hold back but keep it crisp and clear.

Light the tealight and set the boat into the water. Be mindful of your safety but if possible allow it to be placed past the first small waves. Say:

"I know you hear me! ... my wish comes to you!"

Watch as your boat of wishes travels towards Yemaya. Watch it bobbing up and down over the waves glowing in the dusk until she takes it below the sea to her.

Express your gratitude as she will now grant your wish! Act upon any ideas you may have that come to mind to hasten this.

CONNECTING WITH DIVINE ANIMALS

Just like working with gods and goddesses, connecting with the energies of animals enables us to deepen our magic and boost its effectiveness. There are many animals linked specifically to the cycles of the moon (and of the earth) and to the lunar deities. Animals such as hares, dogs, wolves, cats, bats, stags, and other creatures of the night can lend us their energies when we play under the moon.

Familiars on the other hand are animals you have a particularly close relationship with, similar to the way in which US First Nations tribes use animal totems. These familiars guide, teach, warn and protect. Animals, in particular cats, hares and stags, have been historically linked with witches and the craft over the centuries. Creatures that assisted witches closely with their energies were called familiars. For most of us that is a cat or dog or bird or another animal that lives intimately with us. Within the craft of the wise, animals are used to lend their particular energies to magic. They give us a deeper connection to the powers of the natural world.

I was only a small girl when my grandmother sat with me in bed and we looked out the window into the night and we talked about the sounds and the creatures out there.

I wasn't scared. I was curious. I couldn't see the animals but I sure could hear their voices and their movements. I was a bit sad I couldn't see them, and my gran suggested that I could actually see the hare on the moon. It is one of my oldest memories looking up and seeing that indeed there was a celestial bunny looking down upon me.

And as I grew up, my love of animals grew too and so did my realisation that there was a spiritual energy to them. So it was, too, that I learned about the nature of gods and goddesses through their stories and through their animal natures, before understanding more completely about their spiritual aspects. The hare in some ways started me on this journey of the moon.

The hare is one of the most commonly connected animals to the moon. Hare magic has always been linked to the lunar cycle and the fertility cycle of women. For those who wish to achieve a pregnancy, call in hare magic to help you conceive or balance your cycle (see more about this in the section on the lunar return earlier in the book). For those who are not interested in reproduction, hare magic can be used to quicken up the pace of an outcome or to increase your connection with other cycles like the moon.

The constellation 'Lepus' is also a hare.

One of my favourite myths featuring the hare is that of Èostre, the Goddess of Spring. She and her hare were walking at dawn on a crisp morning at the beginning of spring. The morning was very beautiful, yet still cold, as the winter snows were yet to melt completely.

As they walked they came upon a small bird dying in the cold of the freezing but melting snow. Èostre picked up the small bird distressed at its condition. She held the tiny soul in her hands, trying to revive and warm it, but its life was too far gone to save. Feeling love and pity for the creature, Èostre transformed the bird back into an egg, giving it a chance to be born again.

She placed the egg upon the earth and it hatched. Out came another hare, a mate for her companion and the three of them continued their journey.

Invocation with the Hare

You can do this invocation on any part of the lunar cycle but on the nights you can see the hare clearly (the larger waxing moons) are especially lovely.

Get comfortable and take a few deep breaths.

If you like, open a circle.

Close your eyes and allow your body to rest completely.

Imagine you are lying in a big field with long soft grass. The light is golden and going into the blues of true twilight.

There is a big, full moon rising.

You see the hare in the moon.

You allow the energy of the moonlight and of the lunar hare to enter you. Feel the moon's beams enter you and light up every cell.

Allow this feeling of renewal and power to enter every single cell. Enjoy this feeling, take your time.

You notice some movement in the grass and you first see a pair of ears. Big ears. And another. Soon you realise there are two big hares in the field. They are not looking at you or paying you any attention.

They are engrossed in each other, they are circling each other and they soon rise up on their hind legs.

They begin to swirl and dance, hop and play like they are the only beings in the world.

They leap higher, spin faster. Then you hear their voices sing:

> "We aren't mad
> We are dancing
> We are spinning
> Because we are blissful
> We wait for the moon
> To cycle round to wonder
> Our blood tells us
> Where the weaving begins."

We ask the hares to bless us with fertility and with freedom.

We feel this in every cell. We stand, we become the hares dancing.

We feel this powerful energy of being one with all and being able to create anything!

The hares begin to slow their dance.

They look so beautiful under the moonlight. They now lower themselves into the grass and hop away.

You thank the hares.

You keep the feeling of joy and blood rush but it's time to return.

You become aware of your presence in your room or wherever you are.

You return.

When you are ready you stretch and open your eyes.

Close your circle if you opened one.

Welcome back, traveller!

Finding Your Animal Guide Ceremony

It is always better to experience discovering your own magical animal companion if you can. As I said in the beginning, experientially learning is better than me telling you what your lunar animal might be.

I suggest you do this ceremony on both a dark and full moon. You will most likely meet different animals.

You might like to record this on your phone first and play it back or I have a version of this to music you can download through the store on my website.

Have a ritual bath. (Bath with a handful of salt and herbs/flowers of your choice.)

Dress comfortably.

Lay on the floor or bed.

Open a circle if you wish.

Ensure that you are warm and comfortable.

Close your eyes and centre yourself.

Breathe deeply and slowly.

Feel yourself breathing into the floor.

Beginning with your big toe, flex and relax each and every part of your body slowly one by one. Allow yourself to feel the muscles and bones stretch as you relax.

Visualise all the stress and tension running out of them. Even imagine your hair stretching and relaxing. You may notice some places of tension or worries you have keep popping up. Notice them and set them aside to come back to later.

Imagine you are lying on a bed of the softest grass. Every breath relaxes you deeper and deeper onto the grass. It is unbelievably soft. Like ribbons of satin. You are so, so relaxed and comfortable. You can feel the warm sun on your face and body. Mmmm.

You can hear the sound of a small creek or river. The soft babbling is making you even more relaxed. You can see the creek. You stand and walk down to the bank. You are barefoot and the grass is soft against the bottoms of your feet. The water you have now reached is cool and sparkling. Bend down and drink from it if you wish. It is so fresh and clean. How delicious!

Now, it is time to leave behind those tensions and worries that you noticed before. You are going to put them in the river. It is safe to do so. Watch as the pure energy of the water washes your problems and your stress away. Watch them being carried far away from you by the current.

Now, you are ready to meet your guide.

Notice, to one side is a path that you did not see before. Follow it. As you walk, notice that there are many sounds and smells around you. Take in the whole vista of the earth, of the water, and of the sky. Take your time and enjoy this as these are your kindred, your sisters and your brothers. Continue to walk along the path.

The path is now starting to enter a forest. As you walk the canopy is getting thicker and thicker, blocking the sunlight. There are eyes of all shapes and sizes watching you from the shadows. Some are large. Some small. It is much quieter now. You can hear the sound the wind makes as it rustles through the trees.

Notice how you are feeling. Are you afraid? Are you calm? Are you excited?

What are you feeling?

Continue walking, the path is still clear for you. There is nothing here that can do you harm. You are safe.

Ahead, you see some light. You are coming out of the forest now into a clearing. You are in a circular area surrounded by trees, rocks and water. The sun is shining here and when you look up the sky is boundlessly blue.

Sit at the edge of this circle. You are here to meet someone.

Ask:

| *"Come. Will you come?"*

Now wait. Look around, above and below, for signs of your guide. Ask again if necessary.

| *"I am here. I am waiting. Will you come?"*

Take your time, there is no hurry. You will see your guide or guides. They will enter the circle.

Notice its appearance, its special strengths and its markings. How does it move? Is it making any noise?

Staying seated, will it approach you? Will it allow you to touch it? How close can you get?

If your guide welcomes you to touch it, then gently stroke it, talk to it, and play with it. Take your time. This is an important time.

Does your guide have a message for you at this time? Listen. If so, thank your guide. If not, know there may be one at a later time.

If your guide seems willing, ask if you could become one with it, if you can shapeshift with your guide. If not, accept this.

If you feel shapeshifting is allowed, look into the eyes of your guide, and begin to see what it would see, from its height, from its viewpoint.

Listen now for your guide's heartbeat. Breathe deeply and hear yours. The two rhythms are different at first but now slowly they are moving to one rhythm.

Your bodies now are moving towards each other, closer and closer, until suddenly you are inside the skin of your guide. Feel the power of the muscles inside that body. Stretch! Move! Experience how different it is from yours.

Begin to hear what it may hear. Perhaps it hears more than you and you can hear the tiniest whisper of leaves brushing together.

Smell what it can smell. If you feel it is allowed, move around, run, fly, jump as your new shape. How does it feel?

What possibilities are there in this body?

When you are ready, choose to venture back to the circle. It is now time to take back your human form. Say your name and begin to visualise your guide outside of your body.

Thank your guide. Say your goodbyes. Again, take your time. Now is the time to leave a small gift. This could be a piece of food, shelter, anything you think your guide will appreciate.

Always know you can come back to this place whenever you wish and meet with the guide you have met, or any other who has a message for you.

Leave the circle by the path and walk back the way you have come. If you wish to pick up any of your stress and problems at the river, do so, but you are probably feeling so relaxed and secure that they can stay there.

When you are ready, lay down again on your bed of soft grass. Begin to wake up every part of your body one part at a time until you have surfaced in this world again.

Say your name three times out loud and ground yourself further should you need to.

Close your circle if you opened one.

Feel blessed if you met your consultant and/or guide today! Take heed of their message and their medicine.

If you did not meet your guide this time, know that you have established the path to the place where you can meet them another day.

Guides will appear when they are ready.

Blessing Your Animal Companion Ritual

This is a very sweet and joyful blessing involving the Japanese god Jizo for your pets or familiar. If your pet has a collar or favourite toy or blanket you can bless this object. If your animal is around when you cast, simply place a hand upon them to connect.

This should be performed on a full or new moon.

You'll need:

- A candle
- Bell
- Incense
- The items you want blessed (optional)

Light the candle and incense.

Bow once. Say:

> *"Jizo,*
> *I ask that you show your gentle smile to me*
> *I ask that you hold your hand out to me*
> *I ask that your comforting energy be present."*

> *"Jizo (ring a bell or rattle)*
> *I am so grateful I have animal companions who share my space and who love me and I them.*
> *I would ask that they never suffer and that they walk protected and within love."*

> *"Jizo (ring a bell or rattle)*

Please bless this (collar, blanket, etc.)
And empower it with protection, support, comfort and love.
You who relieve all suffering and show a path of light
Embody this (collar etc.) with your blessing.
Thank you, Jizo." (ring bell or rattle)

Blow out the candle.

Other Ways to Connect with Your Divine Animal(s)

1. Draw a picture of your favourite animal/animals or find a picture of your animal and put it up in your home.

2. Learn as much as you can scientifically about your animal through books, documentaries or through watching them in nature.

3. Write devotionals/poems/songs about your animal and keep notes about them in your own special place/altar.

4. Ask for your animal to visit you in your meditations and dreams to give you a special message or lesson.

5. Relax and imagine yourself walking through a green grassy field, sit down and see yourself being met by your animal. Ask in your mind what it is that you need to learn or see from this animal. Be as clear as you can.

6. GET OUTSIDE and reconnect with nature. This increases your ability to connect to the energies of nature and thus with the energies of non-humans.

7. Through invocation and ritual.

8. Creating talismans and amulets often using the fur/feathers/scales etc. of the animal. (These are found substances only.)

If you want some further guidance about particular animals and the way they can be used in magic perhaps my oracle deck 'Divine Animals' might give you some detailed assistance. It deeply engages with over 40 animals and their mythos and symbology.

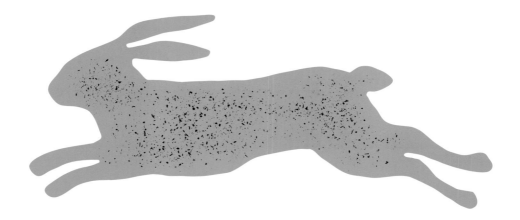

LUNAR ENERGIES AND CRYSTALS

U tilising crystals to focus on and capture energy is something that many practitioners, both pagan and non-pagan, practise. One of the most popular ways of cleansing and charging your crystals is to place them under the moonlight, usually at the full moon.

However, there are some subtle ways of enhancing the energies of crystals by matching the specific lunar energy at certain times in the cycle or even by using solar energy instead.

There are three processes I wish to share when it comes to crystals and the lunar cycle.

The first is **cleansing** which is the clearing of energy within the crystal or stone which of course you should do if buying a new crystal or preparing it for dedication or spell work.

The second is **dedication** which is magnifying the energy for a specific purpose magically. In some ways, it's like telling the crystal what you would like it to do or help you with specifically. We use crystals these days for many things – talismans, in grids, mandalas, in juju bags and more – so it is important that we start them off and point the energy in the right direction.

The third is **charging** which means passing energy through the crystal and enlivening it. Although many people believe that crystals embody their own energy and that is enough, I understand things a little differently. I see them as a kind of filter that the energy runs through and is stored within. Like quartz in a watch, they regulate and send out a particular frequency and vibrancy. If we expose the crystal to flowful, active energy – say energy we draw up from the earth ourselves or the lunar energies, we increase that volume of energy that is passing through – like an electric current. This turbo charges their effectiveness.

Placing your stones where the moonlight arcs as uninterrupted as possible through the night for the longest is the best strategy. If I am placing them on a table or manmade item I put a soft cloth down first, but if I am placing on the earth (natural stone, grass, moss, even in trees), I keep the connection natural with no barrier.

If I am dedicating, before placement, I hold the crystal in my hands allowing my own energy to pass through the stone. I then dedicate the crystal by an invocation almost like an instruction. For example:

"Wise stone, I ask that you help me with... balancing my emotions."

Cleansing

Now I'm going to give you plenty of options here.

There are some folk who cleanse their crystals by leaving the crystals out under the power of a big bright full moon. Some, because it's cleansing – reducing what is there – love to leave out their crystal on multiple waning moons up to dark moon.

In my opinion, both work, but I am partial to cleansing on waning through to dark moons and then rededicating on a full moon.

Dedication and Charging

Dedicating for matters of prosperity

I have had success with leaving crystals in a bowl of shallow water out in the moonlight. The water promotes flow of money towards you. This should be done on the waxing cycle from new moon up to full moon. If your prosperity is being affected by something that is draining your finances eg: a bad habit, an old debt, I would also have a separate crystal to help you with that, which has been dedicated under a dark moon.

Dedicating for matters of growth

Place crystals on living soil/plants. Grass is perfect, as is a healthy pot plant. Leave out under moonlight from new moon to full moon. Then leave out for a full day of sunshine too.

Dedicating to absorb negative energies

Many crystals are useful to us in the way that they help us dispel or absorb negative energies. Jet, obsidian, black tourmaline and pink kunzite are good for this purpose. Give these crystals an extra boost by dedicating them or charging them on a dark or waning moon cycle.

Dedicating for meditation or channelling

I very much like to dedicate stones such as lapis, amethyst, clear quartz or turquoise during dark moons when the energies are aligned for more introverted, inward facing activities. I like to take these crystals into the darker parts of my garden or even areas shaded slightly by rocks but still able to be graced by the sky. I try and retrieve them just before dawn to keep the integrity of the 'darkness' intact. They are calm and peaceful stones that keep our groundedness and balance.

Dedicating for love and relationships

Here is your chance to get really clever with your crystals. New moon is the perfect phase to dedicate a stone to the attraction of a new relationship or to renew one. The waxing cycle also strengthens a current relationship or brings a friendship to you. Full moon is great for all aspects but especially for lust and sexual healing. The waning cycle is wonderful for removing obstacles in the way of a great relationship or love (be mindful not to interfere with free will here) and the dark moon is sublime for forgiveness, self-care and self-love.

A small tip re Solar energies

Whilst I love to leave my crystals out basking in the silvery moonlight there are some crystals that thrive under the fiery sun. I find that naturally gold or warm coloured stones like amber and citrine often need a good dose of solar energy to keep them 'happy', so don't be afraid to leave them out on sunny days. When dedicating your crystals, you will still need to cleanse them first in whichever manner works best for you, but here are some charging and dedication suggestions using solar energies that work for me.

Dedicating for health

On three days running from dawn till dusk, leave out your crystals that will be dedicated to health and healing. Mid-summer and the time around the new moon is an ideal time to do this.

Dedicating for inspiration

Get a boost from the biggest fire of all to fan your personal embers of inspiration: the sun. Place your stones on a natural surface, like grass or a plant and leave them out from dawn till dusk for seven days – then under a new moon. Each spring is a great time to do this.

The masculine

When I am giving a crystal to a man, I always leave it out under the sun for a day or so. The sun gives the stone a charging of masculine energy which I believe enables it to bind more quickly to its new owner. For women, leave under the moon instead.

SPECIFIC MOON PHASES AND ASSOCIATED CRYSTALS

Here is a list of the crystals I find really compatible and powerful with particular moon phases. You can use them in gridding or mandalas, on your altar, to boost spells and energy raising, wear them, carry them or pop them in a juju bag.

Stones which are great universals with lunar energy are clear quartz, and Herkimer diamonds and diamonds. Metals include platinum and silver, and pearls – being from the ocean – are also very compatible with lunar workings.

Dark Moon: Jet

New Moon: celestine
Waxing Crescent 1: aventurine
Waxing Crescent 2: lepidolite
Waxing Crescent 3: charoite
Waxing Crescent 4: rose quartz
Waxing Crescent 5: emerald
Waxing Crescent 6: pyrite

First Quarter Moon: azurite
Waxing Gibbous 1: yellow jasper
Waxing Gibbous 2: aquamarine
Waxing Gibbous 3: obsidian
Waxing Gibbous 4: hematite
Waxing Gibbous 5: carnelian
Waxing Gibbous 6: rhodonite

Full Moon: moonstone
Waning Gibbous 1: tiger's eye
Waning Gibbous 2: turquoise
Waning Gibbous 3: bloodstone
Waning Gibbous 4: larimar
Waning Gibbous 5: azurite
Waning Gibbous 6: fluorite

Last Quarter Moon: ocean jasper
Waning Crescent 1: black tourmaline
Waning Crescent 2: red jasper
Waning Crescent 3: orange calcite
Waning Crescent 4: smokey quartz
Waning Crescent 5: amethyst

Two mandalas I like to weave:

Enliven mandalas with your breath and words of energy upon them.
  For example:

"To the north, the south.
The east and to the west,
I blow energy and my life force upon the intention.
Make it so."

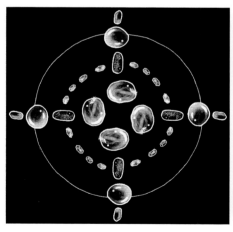 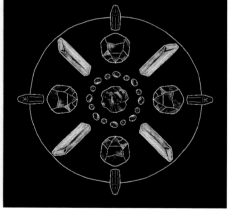

TALISMANS, CHARMS AND AMULETS

The making of talismans, charms and amulets are one of the oldest skills of the witch or shaman of the village and one linked strongly with the moon cycle.

Let's get clear about what does what...

What is an Amulet?

A device that has a purpose of protection by magical means. It can be worn like jewellery or placed on clothing.

What is a Charm?

A charm is for good luck and happiness; protection is not its primary function. It is normally worn on one's person. It could be an object or jewellery – for example, a charm bracelet or a charm on a chain worn around the neck.

What is a Talisman?

A talisman is an object imbibed/charged with magical properties for a particular purpose – power. Some are protective but that's not normally the only function.

Protection from what?

The answer depends on what part of the world you come from: evil eye (in the old days from witches), thieves, bad deeds, jealousy, sickness.

The people that were most in need of these objects were the vulnerable – babies, the old and the sick but also those in transition, those who were moving from one life stage to the next such as pregnant women and brides.

Commonly the shaman, priest or priestess of the village or the wise woman... a grandmother, grandfather, mother... or the person themselves, would make the amulet, charm or talisman and make the magic around it.

Some famous examples of this kind of magic are the warrior swords of Japan and also the swords of the Celts. Both cultures had spiritual practitioners present in the creation and forging of the weapon. It was said the spirit and intention was forged in the sword with prayers and songs sung over the making. When the sword was completed, the song of the sword was activated by the will of the owner, and to enliven it, the last blow on the anvil is the owner's. It was believed too that the weapon, if passed on after death, imbibed the courage, skill and bravery of the past ancestors.

The first action when deciding to do this work is the focus. What will this piece of magic do?

Is it protective? Is it for creativity? For happiness, to attract love, attract money, courage, truth, good... or all of those things? And more? Depending on what that may be, this will determine and shape which way you'll create the magic.

Firstly, I would look at symbology: This links a deeper connection with the purpose of power – what colours suit my amulet or talisman? What goddess or god will I call in to help? Is it suitable to wear or is it more appropriate to carry out of sight? Do I need herbs? What moon phase will assist me best?

The making: However I choose to create the amulet or talisman, as I am making it, just as the Celts did with their swords, I must hold the intention in my mind strongly. This isn't the time when you make something and watch the TV at the same time. You are making magic. For a particular purpose. That is it.

The invocation: This is the part of the magic where you are speaking 'through' the talisman – in other words you are telling it what it should be doing. For example, you might now have a piece of jewellery that you have made which will be a protective piece for someone. You will hold that piece in your hands, raise power and speak the words of power: "I name you as a protective force for my friend Sally. All danger will be repelled, all those who will do her harm shall step back. I ask that the goddess Athena bless me and this amulet of protection, and guide Sally wisely in her journey."

The baking: Here is where you magnify the power of the talisman or amulet. Leaving the piece out under multiple moon cycles under particularly helpful phases is a great way to do this. When I make amulets and talismans, usually it's over a number of moon cycles.

In the case of the example, I would give the talisman a moon charge under the dark and full moons. These extremes cover Sally come what may!

The enlivening: When I have completed the magical work and the 'baking' I enliven the talisman, enabling it to do its magic for the person I have made it for. I hold the talisman in my hands after raising power, and I breathe upon it three times. I then tell it it's 'alive and beautiful'. It's now 'awake' and working.

JUJU BAGS AND POPPETS

A juju bag is a little fabric or leather bag that holds a variety of magical items that are gathered together for a specific reason. Like talismans and amulets they are 'baked' and enlivened.

A typical juju bag might contain certain symbols, written information, something corresponding to an element or deity we might want to engage, and herbs. An incantation will be said over it.

They are then blessed and charged under the appropriate lunar phase or cycle. (See waxing and waning information earlier in the book as a guide.)

Here are some examples of juju bags I have made.

To bring prosperity:

A shell representing the flowful element of water, a trident drawn on paper to represent the god Poseidon who was the richest of the gods, a gold coin, a pinch of dried basil leaves, a piece of citrine.

Blessed under a waxing cycle culminating in a full moon.

For protection:

Some rue leaves, a dried chilli, an arrowhead dedicated to Artemis the Archer, obsidian, a drawing of my patron animal.

Blessed under a dark and new moon.

For happiness:

Marigold petals, calendula petals, an amazonite, a piece of shed hair from my happy dog, a tiny statue of the goddess Hathor (a happy and content goddess!).

Blessed from a new full moon waxing cycle.

A poppet is a little piece of magic, like a juju bag, but it is often formed human shaped. For many people, the first kind of poppets they may think of are voodoo dolls, complete with pins. This means the idea of a poppet automatically gets a negative connotation, when indeed the opposite is true.

Poppets were mentioned as a witches' tool in the famous Malleus Maleficarum (The Hammer of Witches), a guide to the eradication of witches, and was admissible evidence of witchcraft during the Inquisition. The treatise describes how women and men become inclined towards witchcraft and how poppets may be used.

The authors argued that women were more susceptible to demonic temptations through the manifold weaknesses of their gender. It was believed that they were weaker in faith and more carnal than men. Historians claim that most of the women accused as witches had strong personalities and were known to defy convention by overstepping the lines of proper female decorum and often they were the women of the village who were healers or who were seen gathering herbs at night by the moon.

Poppets have been used in magic, particularly magic to promote health and love, for a very long time. They are often used to represent a person or oneself for aid or healing. They may be whittled from roots, wood or even potatoes. They may be made from wax, fabric, string, or fabric stuffed with herbs and other goodies.

Poppets DO NOT have to be human shaped although this is common. They can be symbol shaped, geometrical (e.g. square, pillow shaped).

Symbols or decorations are added to poppets and sigils are common.

Always ask permission if you are preparing a poppet that will impact someone else, no matter how benevolently. Remember, the law of free will.

POTIONS

Potions – don't you love the word? Immediately you feel magical and mysterious! Potion making is an extremely old tradition, first created for healing and ritual means.

Almost all cultures are linked with herbal lore and used potions for health, healing and often to change one's state, e.g. hallucinogens, trance inducers, alcohol!

Potions can be for internal and external use. Internal uses are traditionally referred to as elixirs. Topical potions include oils, bath additions, salves and ointments.

Basic Potions Skills

Again, this is all about your intent and lining up the right energies of the moon and the ingredients to all be weaving towards the one purpose.

The first 'potion to learn' is aqua luna. This is simply leaving water out under the full moon to be blessed. You can keep it for a cycle in the fridge in a flask. Aqua luna is great as a base for most things.

Lunar noir is a dark water and is the same as aqua luna but is left out under a dark moon. Great as a base for cleansing and proactive potions or in association with dark goddesses.

You can also make aqua sol the same way but leave the water out under a midday sun. Aqua sol is great for bringing masculine energies to potions or for healing and prosperity.

Like talismanic work, holding one's focus and imbibing the ingredients with intent-filled incantations and energy is key.

Potions with flowers and oils:

Here are some attributes for potion making around some key deities.

FREYJA

Nordic Goddess of Sexuality & Power

Symbols: white cats, amber, feathered cape, sexuality, confidence, seduction

Colours: amber (deep orangey yellow), white

Feeling: sexy, powerful, rich, irresistible

Oils: amber, frankincense, pine

Moon: new or full

ARTEMIS

Greek Goddess of the Hunt, self-hood, focus, freedom

Symbols: arrows, arrowheads, hunting dogs, forest, freedom, independence, self-esteem, self-trust, outdoors

Colours: white, forest green, silver

Feeling: free, fresh, athletic, confident

Oils: pine/juniper, melissa, cedarwood

Moon: new and waxing

ÈOSTRE

Germanic Goddess of Spring, growth, fertility

Symbols: rabbits, birds, flowers

Attributes: fertility, new beginnings, renewal, creation

Colours: pale pink, green, light yellow

Feeling: inspirational, loving, creative, fresh, green

Oils: rose/rose-geranium, orange, May Chang

Moon: new

PELE

Hawaiian Goddess of Volcanoes, awakening

Symbols: fire, flowers, volcanoes, lava

Attributes: expression of emotions, volatile, passion, power

Colours: fiery red, gold

Feeling: exciting, passionate, powerful, earthy, flowing, coveting

Oils: coconut, cinnamon, frangipani, hibiscus

Moon: dark and new

GANESHA

Hindu God, The Remover of Obstacles, wisdom, wealth

Symbols: elephant, mouse, aum

Attributes: remover of obstacles, placer of obstacles, forgiveness, wise

Colours: gold, hot pink, yellow

Feeling: happiness, ease, wise, luxurious

Oils: patchouli, sandalwood, ginger

Moon: waxing cycle

ATHENA

Greek Goddess of Wisdom, Strategy & Protection

Symbols: the owl, war helmet, olives, spear

Attributes: wise, strategic, brave, protective

Colours: white, royal blue

Feeling: confident, powerful, capable, knowledgeable, protected

Oils: lemon, cypress, vetiver, olive, rosemary

Moon: full

DIONYSUS

God of Pleasure, music, dancing, parties!

Symbols: thunderbolt, ivy, wine/grapes

Attributes: joy, pleasure, partying, appreciation
of the good things in life, movement

Colours: ivy green, ox-blood red

Feeling: P-A-R-T-Y, pleasure, ecstasy, spontaneous, freedom

Oils: ylang ylang, bay, bergamot, wormwood

Moon: dark and full

LILITH

Goddess of Feminine Power & Equality

Symbols: the snake

Attributes: standing your ground, strength, triumph over fear, equality

Colours: black, red

Feeling: feminine strength, deep power, fearlessness

Oils: black pepper, myrrh, coriander, apple cider, jasmine

Moon: dark

☽ POSEIDON ☾

God of the Sea

Symbols: horses, ocean, sea horse, trident

Attributes: flow, prosperity, earthquakes, action, fertility

Colours: blue, black, gold, white, red

Feeling: creative, powerful, prosperous, generous

Oils: salt, bay, bladder wrack, olive, rose geranium, lemon

Moon: full and on incoming tide

☽ APOLLO ☾

God of Enquiry, oracles, light, music

Symbols: bow and arrow, the sun, three-legged stool

Attributes: power, music, psychic ability

Colours: white, gold and yellow

Feeling: centred, focused, clear, wise

Oils: cedarwood, olive, orange, rosemary, frankincense, bay, honey

Moon: new

ISIS

Goddess of Mothering, Healing, Magic

Symbols: ankh, outstretched wings, knot of Isis
(tyet), throne hieroglyphic symbol, roses

Attributes: mothering, partnership, healing, marriage

Colours: blue, gold, white

Feeling: loved, powerful, full of healing, compassionate, mothering/mothered

Oils: rose, sandalwood, orange, blue camomile, frankincense

Moon: crescents

Here is one of my favourite potions in the form of a bath and in honour of one of the most famous goddess potion makers, Morgan Le Fae:

Try a little magic yourself with this wonderful healing potion for the bath. This spell is not for pregnant women or children.

Mix this potion the night prior to full moon. Use it in the bath on full moon.

You'll need:

- ◐ 1 tablespoon pure honey
- ◐ Rose or rose geranium petals
- ◐ 3 drops rose or rose geranium essential oil
- ◐ 3 drops sandalwood essential oil
- ◐ 2 drops lavender essential oil
- ◐ 2 tablespoons of olive oil or jojoba oil
- ◐ Fresh rosemary twig – you need about 10 leaves
- ◐ Small ceramic mixing bowl
- ◐ Small potion bottle
- ◐ Purple candle

Place the olive oil in the mixing bowl. Add the essential oils drop by drop. Swirl around gently and enjoy the scent.

Say:

> *"Magic is here, magic is there,*
> *Transform this potion, Morgan the fair."*

Add the oils to the potions bottle. Remove the rosemary leaves from the sprig and add those to the bottle.

Leave the potion bottle out under the moon.

The next day, bring the potion bottle inside. When you are ready that night to run the bath, take a separate bowl out and mix the honey and petals together saying:

> *"Sweet and fragrant,*
> *Healing and light,*
> *Make my body,*
> *Strong and bright."*

Run the bath. As it's running, add the honey mixture. The heat of the water will dissolve it. Then light the purple candle.

Just before you turn off the tap, pour in the potion slowly, saying:

> *"Morgan Le Fae,*
> *I call you tonight,*
> *Weave your magic,*
> *This full moon night."*

Turn off the tap, check the temperature is fine for you and get in. Enjoy the magic and healing!

THE
NEVER-ENDING
LEARNING

Just like the cycles of the moon, our learning and wisdom should continually flow. Should you wish to know more about witchcraft, goddesses and gods, working with mythos, and the moon, check out these resources.

www.themodernwitch.com

My website. It has lots of great free information and more resources. Details on my workshops both in person and online.

www.nasa.gov

NASA! Great for moon and astronomy info.

www.paganawareness.org.au

The largest pagan educational body in the southern hemisphere.

www.timeanddate.com

Accurate moon, seasonal and equinox timings.

www.hellenismos.com

Good resource on the ancient Greek religion.

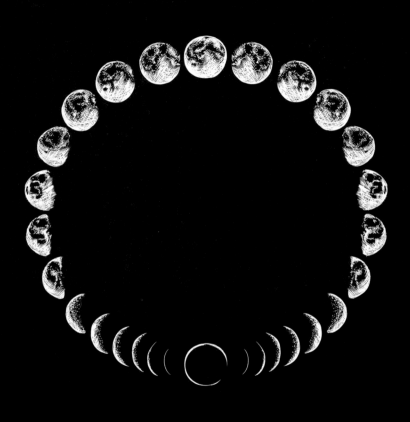

UNIVERSAL DARK, NEW AND FULL MOON CHART

I thought it would be very handy to include this chart listing the three key moon phases for the next 15 years. Happy casting!

Moon Phases chart for 2022–2036

Chart is in UTC (universal time zone)

2022

DARK MOON	NEW MOON		FULL MOON	
1-Jan	2-Jan	18:33	17-Jan	23:48
31-Jan	1-Feb	5:45	16-Feb	16:56
1-Mar	2-Mar	17:34	18-Mar	7:17
31-Mar	1-Apr	6:24	16-Apr	18:55
29-Apr	30-Apr	20:28	16-May	4:14
29-May	30-May	11:30	14-Jun	11:51
28-Jun	29-Jun	2:52	13-Jul	18:37
27-Jul	28-Jul	17:54	12-Aug	1:35
26-Aug	27-Aug	8:17	10-Sep	9:59
24-Sep	25-Sep	21:54	9-Oct	20:54
24-Oct	25-Oct	10:48	8-Nov	11:02
22-Nov	23-Nov	22:57	8-Dec	4:08
22-Dec	23-Dec	10:16		

2023

DARK MOON	NEW MOON		FULL MOON	
			6-Jan	23:07
20-Jan	21-Jan	20:53	5-Feb	18:28
19-Feb	20-Feb	7:05	7-Mar	12:40
20-Mar	21-Mar	17:23	6-Apr	4:34
19-Apr	20-Apr	4:12	5-May	17:34
18-May	19-May	15:53	4-Jun	3:41
17-Jun	18-Jun	4:37	3-Jul	11:38
16-Jul	17-Jul	18:31	1-Aug	18:31
15-Aug	16-Aug	9:38	31-Aug	1:35
14-Sep	15-Sep	1:39	29-Sep	9:57
13-Oct	14-Oct	17:55	28-Oct	20:24
12-Nov	13-Nov	9:27	27-Nov	9:16
11-Dec	12-Dec	23:32	27-Dec	0:33

2024

DARK MOON	NEW MOON		FULL MOON	
10-Jan	11-Jan	11:57	25-Jan	17:53
8-Feb	9-Feb	22:59	24-Feb	12:30
9-Mar	10-Mar	9:00	25-Mar	7:00
7-Apr	8-Apr	18:20	23-Apr	23:48
7-May	8-May	3:21	23-May	13:53
5-Jun	6-Jun	12:37	22-Jun	1:07
4-Jul	5-Jul	22:57	21-Jul	10:17
3-Aug	4-Aug	11:13	19-Aug	18:25
2-Sep	3-Sep	1:55	18-Sep	2:34
1-Oct	2-Oct	18:49	17-Oct	11:26
31-Oct	1-Nov	12:47	15-Nov	21:28
30-Nov	1-Dec	6:21	15-Dec	9:01
29-Dec	30-Dec	22:26		

2025

DARK MOON	NEW MOON		FULL MOON	
			13-Jan	22:26
28-Jan	29-Jan	12:35	12-Feb	13:53
27-Feb	28-Feb	0:44	14-Mar	6:54
28-Mar	29-Mar	10:57	13-Apr	0:22
26-Apr	27-Apr	19:31	12-May	16:55
26-May	27-May	3:02	11-Jun	7:43
24-Jun	25-Jun	10:31	10-Jul	20:36
23-Jul	24-Jul	19:11	9-Aug	7:55
22-Aug	23-Aug	6:06	7-Sep	18:08
20-Sep	21-Sep	19:54	7-Oct	3:47
20-Oct	21-Oct	12:25	5-Nov	13:19
19-Nov	20-Nov	6:47	4-Dec	23:14
19-Dec	20-Dec	1:43		

2026

DARK MOON	NEW MOON		FULL MOON	
			3-Jan	10:02
17-Jan	18-Jan	19:51	1-Feb	22:09
16-Feb	17-Feb	12:01	3-Mar	11:37
18-Mar	19-Mar	1:23	2-Apr	2:11
16-Apr	17-Apr	11:51	1-May	17:23
15-May	16-May	20:01	31-May	8:45
14-Jun	15-Jun	2:54	29-Jun	23:56
13-Jul	14-Jul	9:43	29-Jul	14:35
11-Aug	12-Aug	17:36	28-Aug	4:18
10-Sep	11-Sep	3:26	26-Sep	16:49
9-Oct	10-Oct	15:50	26-Oct	4:11
8-Nov	9-Nov	7:02	24-Nov	14:53
8-Dec	9-Dec	0:51	24-Dec	1:28

2027

DARK MOON	NEW MOON		FULL MOON	
6-Jan	7-Jan	20:24	22-Jan	12:17
5-Feb	6-Feb	15:56	20-Feb	23:23
7-Mar	8-Mar	9:29	22-Mar	10:43
5-Apr	6-Apr	23:51	20-Apr	22:27
5-May	6-May	10:58	20-May	10:58
3-Jun	4-Jun	19:40	19-Jun	0:44
3-Jul	4-Jul	3:02	18-Jul	15:44
1-Aug	2-Aug	10:05	17-Aug	7:28
30-Aug	31-Aug	17:41	15-Sep	23:03
29-Sep	30-Sep	2:36	15-Oct	13:47
28-Oct	29-Oct	13:36	14-Nov	3:25
27-Nov	28-Nov	3:24	13-Dec	16:08
26-Dec	27-Dec	20:12		

2028

DARK MOON	NEW MOON		FULL MOON	
			12-Jan	4:03
25-Jan	26-Jan	15:12	10-Feb	15:03
24-Feb	25-Feb	10:37	11-Mar	1:06
25-Mar	26-Mar	4:31	9-Apr	10:26
23-Apr	24-Apr	19:46	8-May	19:48
23-May	24-May	8:16	7-Jun	6:08
21-Jun	22-Jun	18:27	6-Jul	18:10
21-Jul	22-Jul	3:01	5-Aug	8:09
19-Aug	20-Aug	10:43	3-Sep	23:47
17-Sep	18-Sep	18:23	3-Oct	16:25
17-Oct	18-Oct	2:56	2-Nov	9:17
15-Nov	16-Nov	13:17	2-Dec	1:40
15-Dec	16-Dec	2:06	31-Dec	16:48

2029

DARK MOON	NEW MOON		FULL MOON	
13-Jan	14-Jan	17:24	30-Jan	6:03
12-Feb	13-Feb	10:31	28-Feb	17:10
14-Mar	15-Mar	4:19	30-Mar	2:26
12-Apr	13-Apr	21:40	28-Apr	10:36
12-May	13-May	13:42	27-May	18:37
11-Jun	12-Jun	3:50	26-Jun	3:22
10-Jul	11-Jul	15:51	25-Jul	13:35
9-Aug	10-Aug	1:55	24-Aug	1:51
7-Sep	8-Sep	10:44	22-Sep	16:29
6-Oct	7-Oct	19:14	22-Oct	9:27
5-Nov	6-Nov	4:24	21-Nov	4:02
4-Dec	5-Dec	14:52	20-Dec	22:46

2030

DARK MOON	NEW MOON		FULL MOON	
3-Jan	4-Jan	2:49	19-Jan	15:54
1-Feb	2-Feb	16:07	18-Feb	6:19
3-Mar	4-Mar	6:34	19-Mar	17:56
1-Apr	2-Apr	22:02	18-Apr	3:19
1-May	2-May	14:12	17-May	11:19
31-May	1-Jun	6:21	15-Jun	18:40
29-Jun	30-Jun	21:34	15-Jul	2:11
29-Jul	30-Jul	11:10	13-Aug	10:44
27-Aug	28-Aug	23:07	11-Sep	21:17
26-Sep	27-Sep	9:54	11-Oct	10:46
25-Oct	26-Oct	20:16	10-Nov	3:30
24-Nov	25-Nov	6:46	9-Dec	22:40
23-Dec	24-Dec	17:32		

2031

DARK MOON	NEW MOON		FULL MOON	
			8-Jan	18:25
22-Jan	23-Jan	4:30	7-Feb	12:46
20-Feb	21-Feb	15:48	9-Mar	4:29
22-Mar	23-Mar	3:49	7-Apr	17:21
20-Apr	21-Apr	16:57	7-May	3:39
20-May	21-May	7:17	5-Jun	11:58
18-Jun	19-Jun	22:24	4-Jul	19:01
18-Jul	19-Jul	13:40	3-Aug	1:45
17-Aug	18-Aug	4:32	1-Sep	9:20
15-Sep	16-Sep	18:46	30-Sep	18:57
15-Oct	16-Oct	8:20	30-Oct	7:32
13-Nov	14-Nov	21:09	28-Nov	23:18
13-Dec	14-Dec	9:05	28-Dec	17:32

2032

DARK MOON	NEW MOON		FULL MOON	
11-Jan	12-Jan	20:06	27-Jan	12:52
10-Feb	11-Feb	6:24	26-Feb	7:43
10-Mar	11-Mar	16:24	27-Mar	0:46
9-Apr	10-Apr	2:39	25-Apr	15:09
8-May	9-May	13:35	25-May	2:37
7-Jun	8-Jun	1:32	23-Jun	11:32
6-Jul	7-Jul	14:41	22-Jul	18:51
5-Aug	6-Aug	5:11	21-Aug	1:46
3-Sep	4-Sep	20:56	19-Sep	9:30
3-Oct	4-Oct	13:26	18-Oct	18:58
2-Nov	3-Nov	5:44	17-Nov	6:42
1-Dec	2-Dec	20:52	16-Dec	20:49

2033

DARK MOON	NEW MOON		FULL MOON	
31-Dec	1-Jan	10:16	15-Jan	13:07
29-Jan	30-Jan	21:59	14-Feb	7:04
28-Feb	1-Mar	8:23	16-Mar	1:37
29-Mar	30-Mar	17:51	14-Apr	19:17
28-Apr	29-Apr	2:46	14-May	10:42
27-May	28-May	11:36	12-Jun	23:19
25-Jun	26-Jun	21:07	12-Jul	9:28
25-Jul	26-Jul	8:12	10-Aug	18:07
23-Aug	24-Aug	21:39	9-Sep	2:20
22-Sep	23-Sep	13:39	8-Oct	10:58
22-Oct	23-Oct	7:28	6-Nov	20:32
21-Nov	22-Nov	1:39	6-Dec	7:22
20-Dec	21-Dec	18:46		

2034

DARK MOON	NEW MOON		FLL MOON	
			4-Jan	19:47
19-Jan	20-Jan	10:01	3-Feb	10:04
17-Feb	18-Feb	23:10	5-Mar	2:10
19-Mar	20-Mar	10:14	3-Apr	19:18
17-Apr	18-Apr	19:25	3-May	12:15
17-May	18-May	3:12	2-Jun	3:54
15-Jun	16-Jun	10:25	1-Jul	17:44
14-Jul	15-Jul	18:15	31-Jul	5:54
13-Aug	14-Aug	3:53	29-Aug	16:49
11-Sep	12-Sep	16:13	28-Sep	2:56
11-Oct	12-Oct	7:32	27-Oct	12:42
10-Nov	11-Nov	1:16	25-Nov	22:32
9-Dec	10-Dec	20:14	25-Dec	8:54

2035

DARK MOON	NEW MOON		FULL MOON	
8-Jan	9-Jan	15:03	23-Jan	20:16
7-Feb	8-Feb	8:22	22-Feb	8:53
8-Mar	9-Mar	23:09	23-Mar	22:42
7-Apr	8-Apr	10:57	22-Apr	13:20
6-May	7-May	20:03	22-May	4:25
5-Jun	6-Jun	3:20	20-Jun	19:37
4-Jul	5-Jul	9:59	20-Jul	10:36
2-Aug	3-Aug	17:11	19-Aug	1:00
1-Sep	2-Sep	1:59	17-Sep	14:23
30-Sep	1-Oct	13:06	17-Oct	2:35
30-Oct	31-Oct	2:58	15-Nov	13:48
28-Nov	29-Nov	19:37	15-Dec	0:33
28-Dec	29-Dec	14:30		

2036

DARK MOON	NEW MOON		FULL MOON	
			13-Jan	11:16
27-Jan	28-Jan	10:17	11-Feb	22:08
26-Feb	27-Feb	4:59	12-Mar	9:09
26-Mar	27-Mar	20:56	10-Apr	20:22
25-Apr	26-Apr	9:33	10-May	8:09
24-May	25-May	19:16	8-Jun	21:01
23-Jun	24-Jun	3:09	8-Jul	11:19
22-Jul	23-Jul	10:17	7-Aug	2:48
20-Aug	21-Aug	17:35	5-Sep	18:45
19-Sep	20-Sep	1:51	5-Oct	10:15
18-Oct	19-Oct	11:49	4-Nov	0:44
17-Nov	18-Nov	0:14	3-Dec	14:08
16-Dec	17-Dec	15:34		

ABOUT THE
AUTHOR

Stacey is a best-selling author who specialises in pagan, nature and mythos-based subjects.

She is a witch and pagan educator with works translated into many different languages. She is the author of the popular yearly companion the Lunar & Seasonal Diary for both the southern and northern hemispheres since 2011. Her lunar-based oracle deck *Queen of the Moon* is beloved by moon lovers everywhere.

She is the author of many beautiful oracle decks including *Divine Animal Oracle*, *The Elemental Oracle* and *Moon Magick* mini cards. *Plants of Power* co-written with Miranda Mueller, teaches people how to discover, know and grow some of the most magical and useful plants for healing, eating and transformation.

Stacey lives by the beach on a wild Australian cliff on Sydney's northern beaches in a small house with a big garden with her husband, animal companions and about 10,000 bees – and of course a clear view of the arc of the moon.

You can learn more about Stacey, her workshops, consults and retreats and lunar-based magic by visiting her website www.themodernwitch.com or checking out her social media pages on Facebook and Instagram.